7

BUNNY DROP

yumi unita

STORY

Ten years have passed since Daikichi, a single guy with no experience in child-rearing, made the decision to take in Rin, his grandfather's love child, and create a family life together. For both Rin and Kouki, now high schoolers, and Daikichi and Kouki's mother, the possibility of love for each pair seems to be at an end.

MAIN CHARACTERS

KOUKI NITANI
Rin's childhood friend from daycare. High school first-year. Professed his love to Rin.

NITANI-SAN
Kouki's mother and a single mom. Was proposed to by Daikichi but currently in a holding pattern.

REINA
Daikichi's cousin Haruko's daughter. High school first-year.

MASAKO YOSHII
Rin's birthmother. Manga artist.

MASAKO'S BOYFRIEND
Her lover and chief assistant.

DAIKICHI KAWACHI
Forty years old and single. Used to be like a fish out of water around women and kids but now has an impressive decade of being Rin's guardian under his belt.

RIN KAGA
A smart and responsible high school first-year. Taken in by Daikichi when she was six.

contents

BUNNY**DROP**
episode.37

BUNNY**DROP**

KACHA (CLICK)
カチャ
KACHA
カチャ
KACHA
カチャ
MAA-CHAN, THIS ACCOUNTING SOFTWARE ...
IT'S USELESS. I'M GETTING ANOTHER ONE, OKAY?
SURE ...

WHICH ONE SHOULD WE GET?
I DON'T KNOW. JUST CHOOSE ONE...
OKAY ...
I'M OFF TO THE BANK.
UH-HUH ...
OH.
HER...
...BANK ACCOUNT BOOK TOO...
OH... RIGHT ...
OKAY, THEN I'LL BE BACK AFTER I STOP BY THE BANK AND THE SUPERMARKET.
IF I HAVE TIME, I'LL CHECK OUT SOME ACCOUNTING SOFTWARE.
SURE ...

MANGA: SO WHICH ONE DO YOU LIKE? / IDIOT! / THE MODANYAKI, OF COURSE! / WAIT!

REMEMBER YOU NEED TO TAKE BREAKS, OKAY?
I KNOW ...

RIN, I WANT SOMETHING SWEET.
ME TOO. WHAT SHOULD WE GET?

SO THEN MY DADDY...
YEAH?
OH!!
I JUST REMEMBERED!! GET THIS, RIN!!
MY DADDY...
HUH?
SWITCHING TOPICS?
HE SMELLS THESE DAYS...
SMELLS?
LIKE, KINDA STINKS...
STINKS...
OH...
OKAY...
I GET IT...
I SAW SOMETHING LIKE THAT...
...ON TV BEFORE...
WHAT...?
THAT CURRY-SHTEW THING?
I THINK IT'S DIFFERENT...
IT ACTUALLY SOUNDS KINDA YUMMY.
FOR REAL...?

IT SAID THAT WHEN A GIRL HITS PUBERTY, A GUY WHO'S CLOSELY RELATED GENETICALLY STARTS TO SMELL MORE TO HER... OR SOMETHING LIKE THAT.
ON TOP OF THAT, AS A GIRL GETS OLDER, SHE EVENTUALLY DOESN'T SMELL IT ANYMORE...
WHAT? REALLY?
MY DADDY'S HANDSOME, SO I'M IN SHOCK ABOUT THIS.
DOESN'T DAIKICHI SMELL!?
UM...?
I DON'T KNOW ...
HE SMELLS A LITTLE RIGHT AFTER HE GETS BACK FROM WORK...
BUT I THINK THAT'S PROBABLY THE SAME FOR EVERYONE ...
IT JUST HASN'T BOTHERED ME AT ALL...
'COS YOUR **GENES** AREN'T AS SIMILAR MAYBE?
WELL, DEFINITELY FARTHER AWAY GENETICALLY THAN YOU AND YOUR DAD...
OH...

WELL, GUESS IT DOESN'T REALLY MATTER!!
IT'S NOT LIKE I SEE HIM EVERY DAY.
HA HA...
SO, WHAT WERE WE TALKING ABOUT?
YOUR DAD...
OH, RIGHT, SO MY DADDY, HE...
RIN...
...CAN I SEE YOUR NOTES ON CLASSICAL JAPANESE AFTER SCHOOL?
SURE...
WANT TO COME OVER?
YEAH!!

WHAT?
KOUKI?
HOW'S HE DOING?
UM...
流通道場
GOOD...
I THINK...
DON'T SEE HIM MUCH?
I'M USUALLY WITH REINA, AND HE'S WITH HIS FRIENDS, YOU KNOW, LIKE TAKEUCHI-KUN, SO...

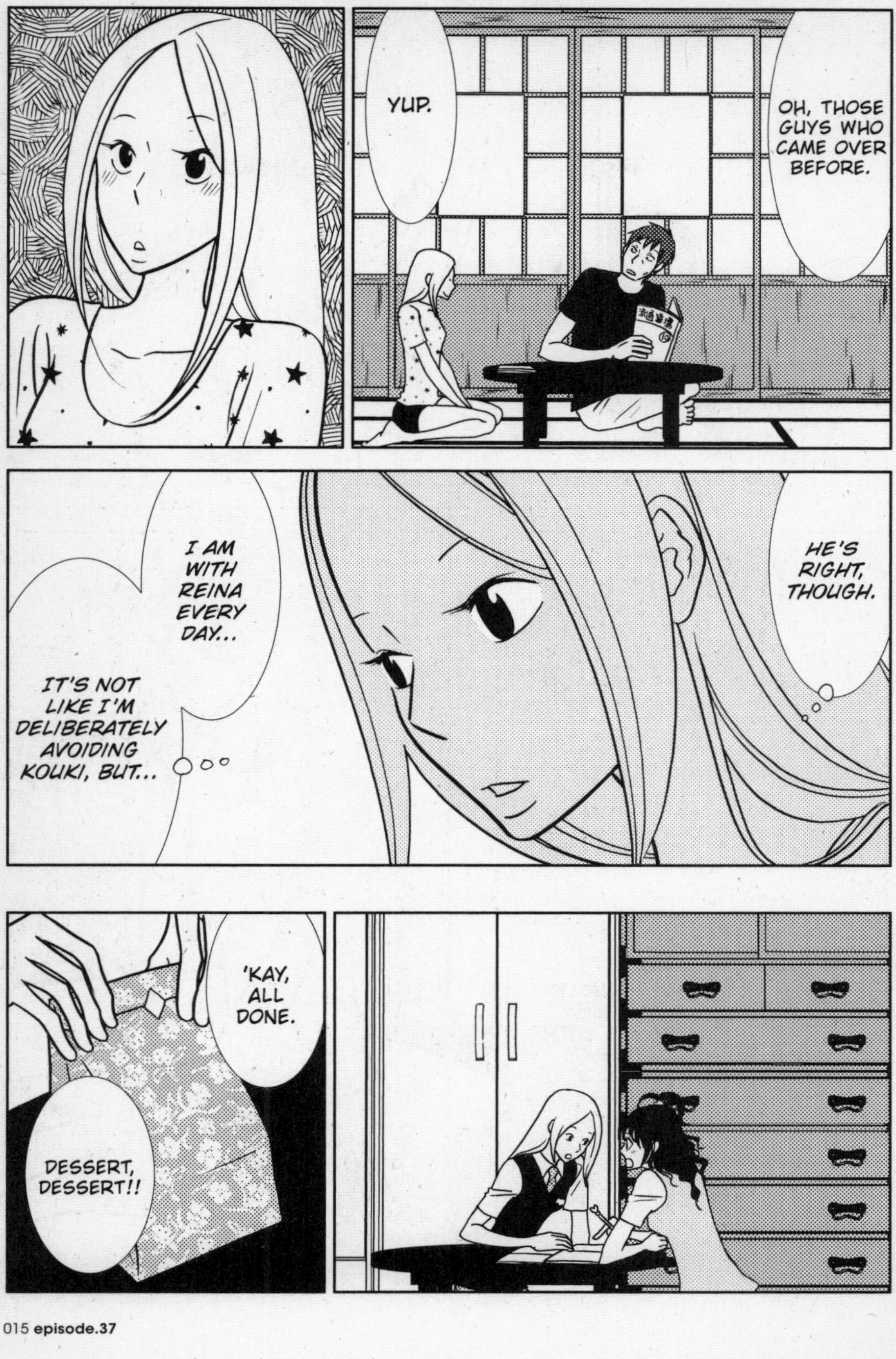
OH, THOSE GUYS WHO CAME OVER BEFORE.
YUP.
HE'S RIGHT, THOUGH.
I AM WITH REINA EVERY DAY...
IT'S NOT LIKE I'M DELIBERATELY AVOIDING KOUKI, BUT...
'KAY, ALL DONE.
DESSERT, DESSERT!!

MUGU (MUNCH)
むぐ
むぐ
MUGU
YOU KNOW ...
...I'M SO GLAD WE GO TO THE SAME HIGH SCHOOL, RIN.
YEAH ...
ME TOO...
EVERYONE STUDIES SO MUCH...
...IT WOULD'VE BEEN LONELY IF I WERE BY MYSELF.
YEAH ...

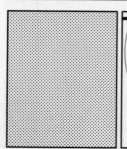

UM...
RIN...
HM?
CAN I TELL YOU SOMETHING ...?
WHAT?
WELL...
UM...
......
WHAT IS IT?
DID SOMETHING HAPPEN, REINA?

I MIGHT ...
...HAVE A BOYFRIEND SOON...
EH!?
REALLY?
SOMEONE FROM SCHOOL?
HEE-HEE... WELL, I DON'T KNOW HOW THINGS'LL GO YET, BUT...
...HE'S A SECOND-YEAR AT OUR SCHOOL AND ON THE BASKETBALL TEAM.
WHA—? HOW DO YOU KNOW PEOPLE LIKE THAT?
OH...
YOU KNOW HOW YOU WENT HOME WHEN THEY HAD THE AFTER-PARTY FOR THE CULTURAL FESTIVAL?
HE CHATTED ME UP A LITTLE THEN...

WOW! REINA, GUY MAGNET!
STOP!!
NO WAY.
WAY. DEFINITELY A GUY MAGNET.
I'VE NEVER HAD SOMEONE I DON'T KNOW CHAT ME UP.
OTHER THAN OLD FOLKS.
WHAT?
REALLY!?
MAYBE THAT'S 'COS KOUKI'S ALWAYS WITH YOU?
BUT WE'RE NOT TOGETHER 24-7...

WHAT!?
REINA!?
A BOY-FRIEND!?
YEAH! SHE MIGHT GET ONE SOON.
APPARENTLY, HE STARTED TALKING TO HER...
...AT THE PARTY AFTER THE CULTURAL FESTIVAL!
REINA'S PRETTY AMAZING, HUH?

AH...
A GUY MAGNET!!
UM...
I'M NOT SURE IF I'D CALL IT AMAZING...
IT'S A PRETTY WORN-OUT MOVE!!
...OR HER A MAG-NET...
BUT WAIT...
HARUKO... WAS PRETTY POPULAR WITH THE GUYS BACK IN THE DAY TOO...I THINK?
OH, REINA'S MOM STILL ATTRACTS THE GUYS NOW TOO!!
'COS SHE'S CUTE!
FOR REAL!!?
THAT'S AMAZ-ING!!
BUT ALL THE ATTENTION SHE GETS IS FROM OLDER GUYS...
OH... OLDER THAN FORTY WOULD BE PRETTY OLD...
AND I GUESS SHE'S SICK OF OLDER MEN, SO IT NEVER GETS REMOTELY CLOSE TO MARRIAGE.
IS THAT SO...?

I WONDER WHY SHE DOESN'T LIKE OLDER GUYS?
WHO KNOWS...
I HAVE NO IDEA SINCE I'VE NEVER BEEN MARRIED.
すん
SUN (SNIFF)
すん
SUN
WH-WHAT THE HECK?
HM?
DO I SMELL?
I CAN'T REALLY TELL...
MAY-BE...
YOU DON'T SMELL THAT BAD.
...I OUGHTA TAKE A BATH BEFORE DINNER FROM NOW ON...
PLUS I'LL GET FAT IF WE EAT TOO LATE.

BY THE WAY, DID YOU GO TO THAT AFTER-PARTY THING?
NOPE.
NAH, I JUST MADE *THAT* THE REASON SO I COULD DUCK OUT AND COME HOME.
THAT STUFF IS BOR-ING.
I'M NOT INTO THINGS LIKE THAT...
OH...
ぽん ぽん
SFX: PON (PAT) PON
I HAVE TO MAKE DINNER AND ALL.
DON'T MAKE IT MY FAULT!!
YOU CAN GO IF YOU WANNA.
ちく ちく...
CHIKU (STITCH)
CHIKU
YOU KNOW, YOU AND KOUKI...
I FEEL LIKE YOU MISSED OUT...

I DON'T WANT YOU OF ALL PEOPLE LECTURING ME ABOUT THAT, DAIKICHI!!
SHUT UP, SHUT UP!
OLD GEEZERS DON'T CARE ABOUT STUFF LIKE THAT ANYMORE!!
YOU AND ME BOTH...
WE'RE HOPE-LESS, HUH?
DON'T KEEP SAYING THAT...

SORRY, RIN.
I HAVE PLANS AGAIN TODAY...
IT'S OKAY...
...WITH THE BASKETBALL GUY?
HEE HEE...
HE'S CUTE...

IS IT BETTER ...
...TO HAVE MORE FRIENDS ...?
SIGN: PUBLIC LIBRARY
......
WELL, IN ANY CASE...
...I'LL GET SOME EXAM STUDYING IN...
...THEN GO GROCERY SHOPPING, THEN GO HOME...
...MAKE DINNER ...
...AND DO SOME SEWING UNTIL DAIKICHI GETS BACK...

AGH!
WHY ARE YOU HERE!?
DON'T GET MAD.
I CAN'T HELP IT.

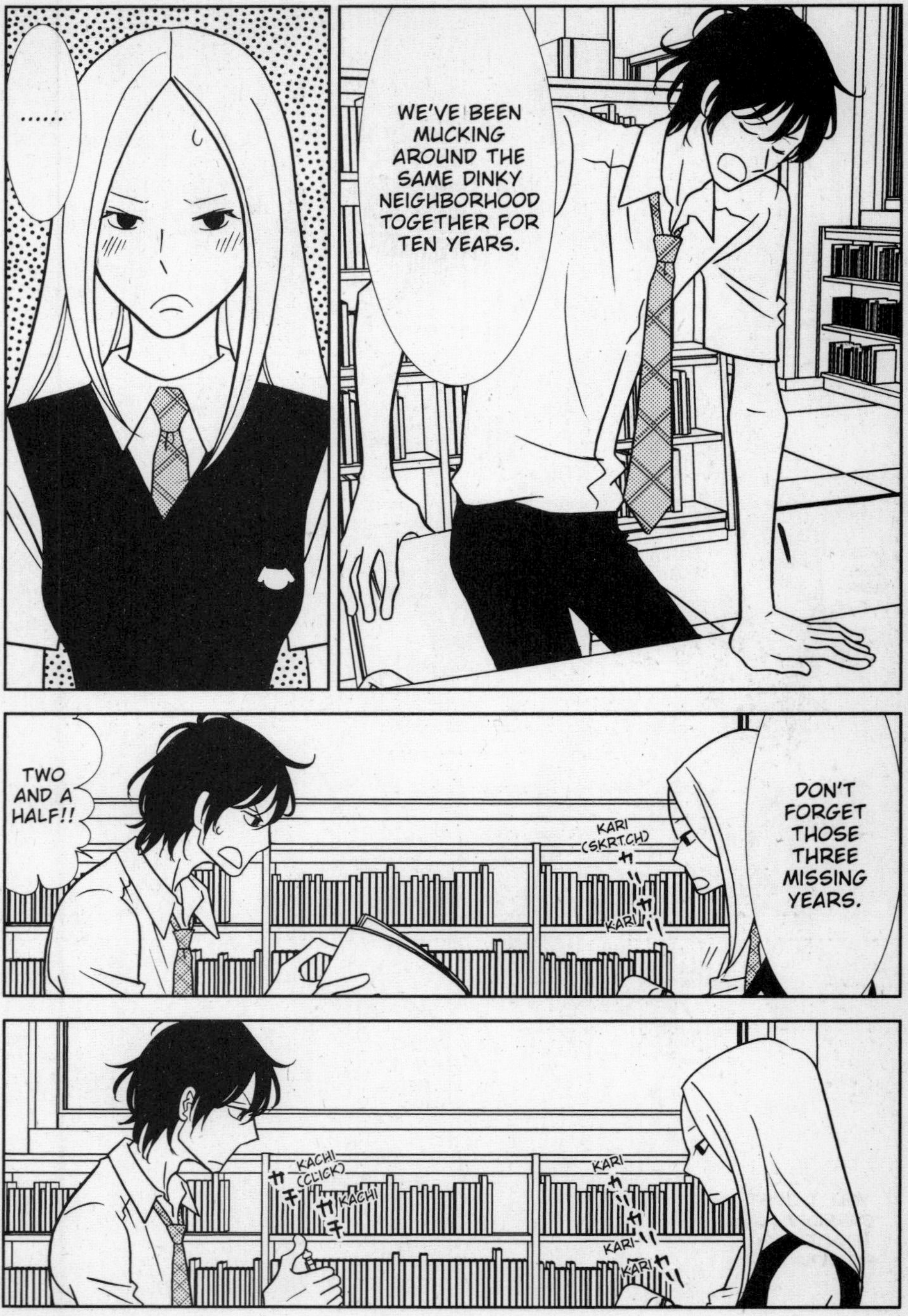
WE'VE BEEN MUCKING AROUND THE SAME DINKY NEIGHBORHOOD TOGETHER FOR TEN YEARS.
......
DON'T FORGET THOSE THREE MISSING YEARS.
KARI (SKRTCH)
KARI
TWO AND A HALF!!
KARI
KARI
KARI
KACHI (CLICK)
KACHI

RIN, HELP ME WITH THIS?
......
WELL... IN THIS CASE...
...SINCE YOU KNOW THE LENGTHS OF ALL THREE SIDES...
...IT'LL BE FASTER TO USE HERON'S FORMULA INSTEAD OF THE LAW OF COSINES TO GET THE ANGLE DEGREES.
YEAH, OKAY...
HERON...
FIRST TIME HEAR-ING IT...
SEE, IT'S RIGHT HERE.
HEY, KOUKI... I GUESS YOU HAVE BEEN STUDYING...
OF COURSE...
...UNLIKE YOU, I JUST BARELY MADE IT INTO HIGH SCHOOL, SO...

NOT TO MENTION, I FIGURE...
...ANY STUDENT LOANS I'M SHOOTING FOR, I'LL HAVE TO PAY BACK EVENTUALLY, RIGHT?
YEAH...
IF I DON'T GET MY ACT TOGETHER...
...JUST LIVING DAY TO DAY WON'T DO ANYTHING FOR MY FUTURE...
UM... SORRY IF THIS IS A TOUCHY SUBJECT, BUT...
HM?
WHAT ABOUT ASKING YOUR DAD TO HELP WITH STUFF LIKE THAT...?

OH.
YOU MEAN CHILD SUPPORT?
... YEAH ...
I HEARD NOT EVERYONE GETS THAT.
YOU CAN'T PAY OUT WHAT YOU DON'T HAVE, RIGHT?
AND ANYWAY, MOM MADE MORE THAN HE DID.
AH...
PLUS IT'S A MOOT POINT IF MOM SAYS SHE DOESN'T WANT IT...
DID I EVER TELL YOU?
I HAVEN'T SEEN MY DAD ONCE SINCE THE DIVORCE.
DON'T REMEMBER A SINGLE THING ABOUT THE GUY.

SO FOR ME, IT WOULD BE LIKE GETTING A HANDOUT FROM SOME STRANGE DUDE.
I'D RATHER FIGURE THINGS OUT ON MY OWN.
HOW ABOUT YOU, RIN?
WELL ...
...DAIKICHI KEEPS TELLING ME NOT TO WORRY ABOUT IT, BUT...
THE SAME GOES FOR DAIKICHI'S MOM AND DAD...

GOOD ...
I'M GLAD ...

HEY.
WHERE ARE TAKEUCHI-KUN AND MATSUMOTO-KUN?
HM?
OH, THEY HAVE CLUB STUFF TO DO AFTER SCHOOL.
THEY DO IT REALLY CASUALLY, THOUGH.
OH...
OKAY...
WHAT ABOUT REINA?
OH... REINA HAS A BOY-FRIEND...
!!!
SERI-OUSLY!?
EVEN THOUGH SHE'S AN AIR-HEAD!?

AH.
THAT'S WHY YOU'RE ALL ALONE.
WHICH IS IT ...?
SHE REALLY IS AN AIRHEAD...
SHE SAID SHE *MIGHT HAVE ONE.*
LOOK WHO'S TALK-ING!!
YOU HAVE, LIKE, NO FRIENDS!

KON
KON (KNOCK)
UGH...
WHAT?

RIN, WILL YOU HURRY UP AND FIND A GUY ALREADY?
IT'S MAKING IT HARD FOR ME.
KA KA KA KA KA (KICK)
RIGHT BACK AT YOU!!
OUCH! OUCH!

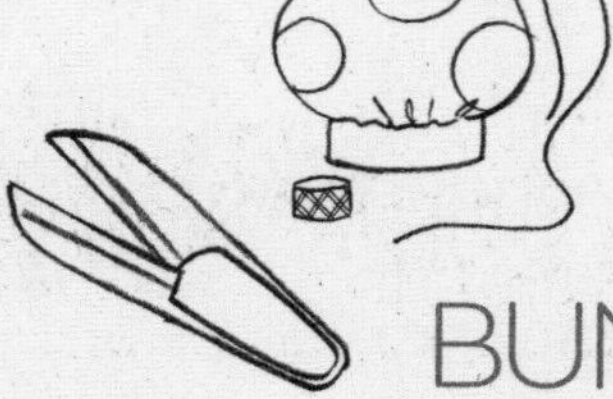

BUNNY**DROP**

BUNNYDROP
episode.38

WANT ME TO DO IT?
IT'S OKAY. I'M ALMOST DONE.

JUST ...
...A LITTLE MORE.
BE CAREFUL.
IT'S FINE.
AH!
I HAVE A LONGER REACH, SO MAYBE I SHOULD—
HUH?
AH!
HEY, WHOA!
WAAAH!

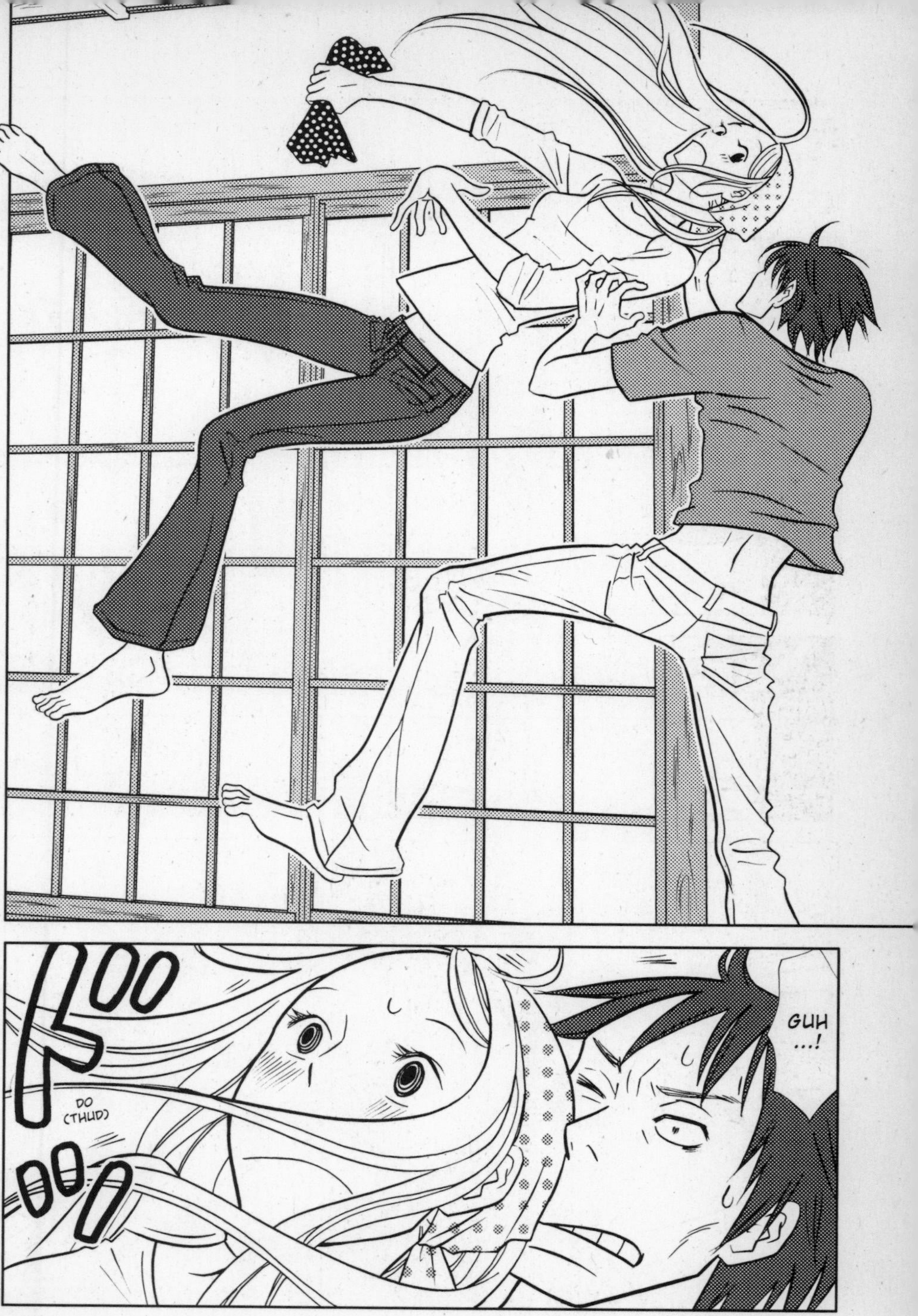
DO (THUD)
GUH ...!

AH?
AH...
AH...
AH...
THAT WAS CLO—
WHEW ...
PASA (FLUTTER)
SORRY, MY HAIR...
AHHH-CHOOO!!

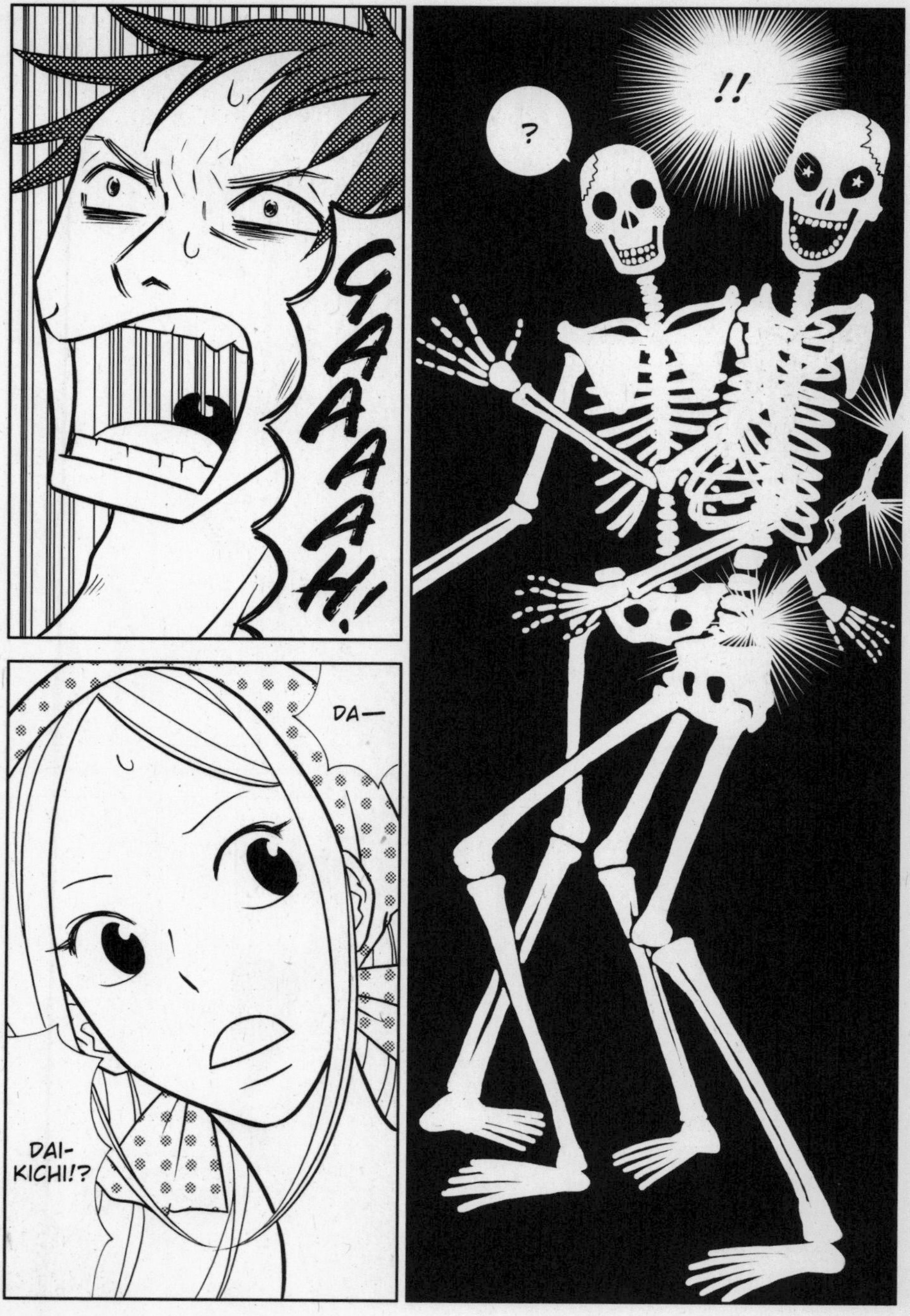
GAAAAAAH!
?
!!
DA—
DAI-
KICHI!?

......
HEY...
WHAT'S WRONG?
DAI-KICHI...
......
I'M... FINE...
FINE...
YOU DON'T SEEM FINE AT ALL!!
I PROB-ABLY... YEAH...
...KINDA STRAINED MY BACK...
!!!

LIKE WHAT HAPPENS... TO GRAND-PAS AND STUFF...?
THIS CAN HAPPEN TO PEOPLE IN THEIR TWENTIES TOO!
YEAH ...
AT LEAST LIE DOWN ON YOUR SIDE!
......
I NEED TO PUT THE FUTON DOWN, SO MOVE OVER.
I WAS JUST ABOUT TO!!
DAMMIT ...AM...
...I GETTING OLD...?
......

THIS IS DE-PRESS-ING...
URGH...
LEAN THIS WAY.
NO!!
I CAN'T!!
WHY NOT?
NO WAY!!
NO!!
'COS MY MOM IS A BUSY-BODY.
SHOULD I CALL YOUR PARENTS?
I JUST GOTTA STAY STILL.
WHAT CAN I DO...?
I DON'T HAVE THE BALLS TO EVEN TRY.
...I PROLLY CAN'T TURN OVER EITHER...
BUT...
DOES IT HURT EVEN WHEN YOU'RE LYING DOWN?
IT'LL BE MORE STRESS-FUL WITH HER HERE...
I'M FINE AS LONG AS I DON'T MOVE.

AAAGH...
PA-THETIC...
EMOTIONALLY, THIS STINGS, BUT...
IN APPAREL BUT DOING SPORTS-ORIENTED MERCHANDISE.
ON TOP OF THAT, DOING OUTGOING SHIPPING.
...A STRAINED BACK AT MY JOB IS LIKE A MATTER OF LIFE OR DEATH...
WITH THE ACTUAL NUMBER OF WORKING DAYS ON THE RISE YEARLY WHILE THE NUMBER OF STAFF STAYS THE SAME, WE'RE ALREADY IN A CRUNCH...
......
THIS IS KINDA SCARY...
CAN I MAKE IT TO RETIREMENT?
CAN I CARRY CARDBOARD BOXES TILL THAT AGE?
DAIKICHI, CAN YOU DRINK WATER?
HMM...
I CAN'T MOVE...

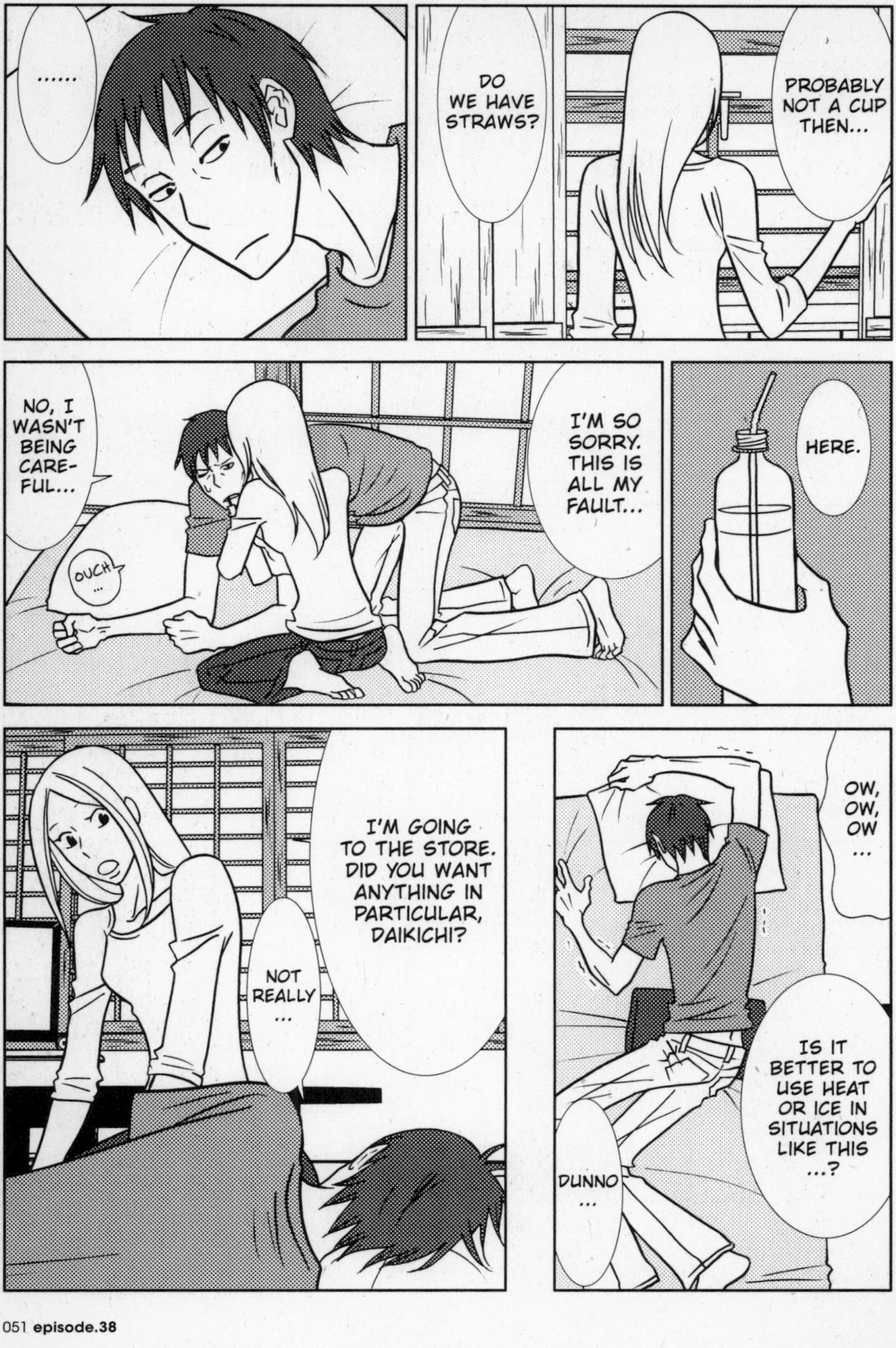
PROBABLY NOT A CUP THEN...
DO WE HAVE STRAWS?
......
HERE.
I'M SO SORRY. THIS IS ALL MY FAULT...
NO, I WASN'T BEING CARE-FUL...
OUCH...
OW, OW, OW...
IS IT BETTER TO USE HEAT OR ICE IN SITUATIONS LIKE THIS...?
DUNNO...
I'M GOING TO THE STORE. DID YOU WANT ANYTHING IN PARTICULAR, DAIKICHI?
NOT REALLY...

OH, HELLO, THIS IS RIN. HOW ARE YOU?
I'M CALLING KOUKI'S.
AH!
WHAT!?
HEY, I TOLD YOU NOT TO CALL MY MOM!!
OHH ...?
OKAY...
YES ...
AH... SO I SHOULD ICE IT FIRST...
...THEN A COLD COMPRESS SHOULD WORK, AND...
I SOUND SO LAME.
NOT GOOD!!
GREAT.
ACTUALLY I WAS CALLING 'COS DAIKICHI PULLED SOMETHING IN HIS BACK...
I GOT NOTHING TO SAY...
HERE.
SHE SAID SHE WANTS TO TALK TO YOU.
THANK YOU SO MUCH. I'LL DO MY BEST.
KILL ME NOW ...

'KAY, WELL, I'M GOING GROCERY SHOPPING NOW!
HELLO...
WHAT'S WITH THAT SMILE?
Does it hurt much?
UM, YES...
IT HURTS...
PLEASE KEEP VERY STILL.
THE BEST THING WOULD BE TO STAY PRONE IN THE MOST COMFORTABLE POSITION.
WELL... I CAN'T MOVE, SO...I'M LYING DOWN NOW...
IT'S BORING.
RIGHT...
If the pain gets worse, make sure to take a shower and not a bath.
No sake either.

Oh... So beer's fine?
I'M SAYING NO ALCOHOL!!
OKAY, OKAY...
...I'LL SEND KOUKI OVER ONCE HE GETS HOME.
HE CAN HELP WITH WHATEVER YOU NEED DONE.
AH...
KOUKI'S COMING ...?
OH! WHAT ARE YOU GETTING AT!?
YOU KNOW FULL WELL I SHOULDN'T BE GOING OVER THERE!
Meh... True...

IF YOU CAN ACT LIKE A SPOILED CHILD THIS EASILY...
...I WISH YOU'D DONE IT MUCH SOONER.
LIKE TEN YEARS AGO.
IF IT CAME TO ME EASY, I WOULDN'T BE HAVING SO MUCH TROUBLE.
I'D HAVE A BUNCHA WIVES ALREADY.
Stop ...
I'M SORRY, I'M SORRY... I WON'T ACT LIKE THAT AGAIN...
BUT GEEZ... HEARING HER VOICE WHEN I'M FEELING LOW...
...I CAN'T HELP ACTING LIKE A BRAT...
...MAKES ME WANNA TEASE HER A BIT...
ごり
GORI (CRACK)

D'OW-OW-OW-OW-OW!!
REALLY I'M SORRY ...
DAIKICHI, HERE YA GO!
THIS ONE HAS GAMES...
...A PSP AND TEKKEN.
AND THIS IS FROM MY MOM...
...FOOD, I THINK ...
VIDEO GAMES?
THAT'S MORE IMPORTANT?
SORRY, THANKS... I'M JUST BORED OUTTA MY MIND.
OH, TELL ME HOW MUCH I OWE YOU FOR THE GAMES.
MOM ALSO SHOWED ME SOME COMFY SLEEPING POSITIONS FOR YOU.
RIN, CAN YOU PUT THE TOWEL UNDER HIS LOWER BACK?
OW, OW, OW ...
OKAY.
DAIKICHI, RELAX AND ROLL THIS WAY.

OKAY ...
I'M NOT SURE HOW TO FEEL ABOUT THIS SITUATION ...
TO THINK THESE TWO WOULD BE TAKING CARE OF ME...
AGH!
DAM-MIT!
WHAT THE HECK ...!
...DAIKICHI, YOU'RE PRETTY GOOD!!
DON'T WRITE OFF THE FAMICON GENERA-TION.
TEKKEN IS MY GAME.
I THOUGHT IT WAS JUST MARIO.
IT'S LIKE THEY'RE FATHER AND SON...
DAIKICHI, PLAY MONSTER HUNTER WITH ME TOO.
NO WAY. IT TAKES TOO LONG.
べた
べた
BETA
BETA (SMACK)
GET AWAY FROM ME.... YOU'RE TOO WARM.
OR MAYBE THIS IS SOMETHING YOU'D NEVER SEE BETWEEN PARENT AND CHILD...?

GOOD EVENING.
EXCUSE US, MAY WE COME IN?
?
AH.
THE GUYS FROM WORK SAID THEY'D BE STOPPING BY TODAY.
COMING!
AH... KAWACHI-SAN LOOKS AFTER US AT WORK, AND US GUYS...UH... WE...
PLEASE COME IN.
UNAGI DROP

SORRY ABOUT THIS. I'LL BE AT WORK TOMORROW.
NO PROBLEM. YOU TAKE THE TIME AND REST UP.
BUT MORE IMPORTANTLY, HOW THE HECK DID RIN-CHAN GET SO PRETTY!?
COMPLETELY DIFFERENT FROM MY IDIOT SON.
OOPS FORGOT ONE SOCK, DUH.
UHH, WELL, SHE'S A DAUGHTER...
BUT THIS BACK SPRAIN THING...
...IT GETS YOU PRETTY LOW...
WELL, IT'S NO WONDER WITH THE EXTRA SHIPMENTS THIS MONTH.
I'VE NEARLY THROWN MY BACK A LOAD'A TIMES TOO...
THANK YOU...
REALLY ...?
WHEN MY KID WAS A BABY...
HUH...
...IT GETS TO YOUR BACK IF YOU DON'T USE THE CRIB RIGHT...
GYAAAAH!
IT HAPPENED TO YOU TOO, DIDN'T IT?
YEAH.
THOSE STROLLERS JUST AREN'T COMFORTABLE... AND SINCE I ALWAYS HAD TO BEND OVER...
!!!

AND ANOTHER HIDDEN CULPRIT IS THAT LINTEL.
BENDING OVER EACH TIME, DAY IN AND DAY OUT, ACTUALLY PUTS A LOT OF STRAIN ON THE BACK.
YOU DUCK WHEN YOU PASS UNDER IT TOO, RIGHT, KAWACHI-SAN?
YEAH, JUST A LITTLE.
OH.
IT'S PROBABLY HARD FOR YOU TO GET UP TO GO TO THE BATHROOM, KAWACHI-SAN.
WANNA GO WITH ME NOW?
SORRY, YEAH.
AH, AND I KNOW A GOOD DOCTOR. WANT ME TO REFER YOU?
YEAH, THANKS.

PAPER: RIN KAGA, DAIKICHI, THE MEAT-AND-POTATO STEW THAT DAIKICHI MAKES IS SO DELICIOUS. AND DAIKICHI CAN RUN REALLY FAST AND IS GOOD AT JUMP ROPE.

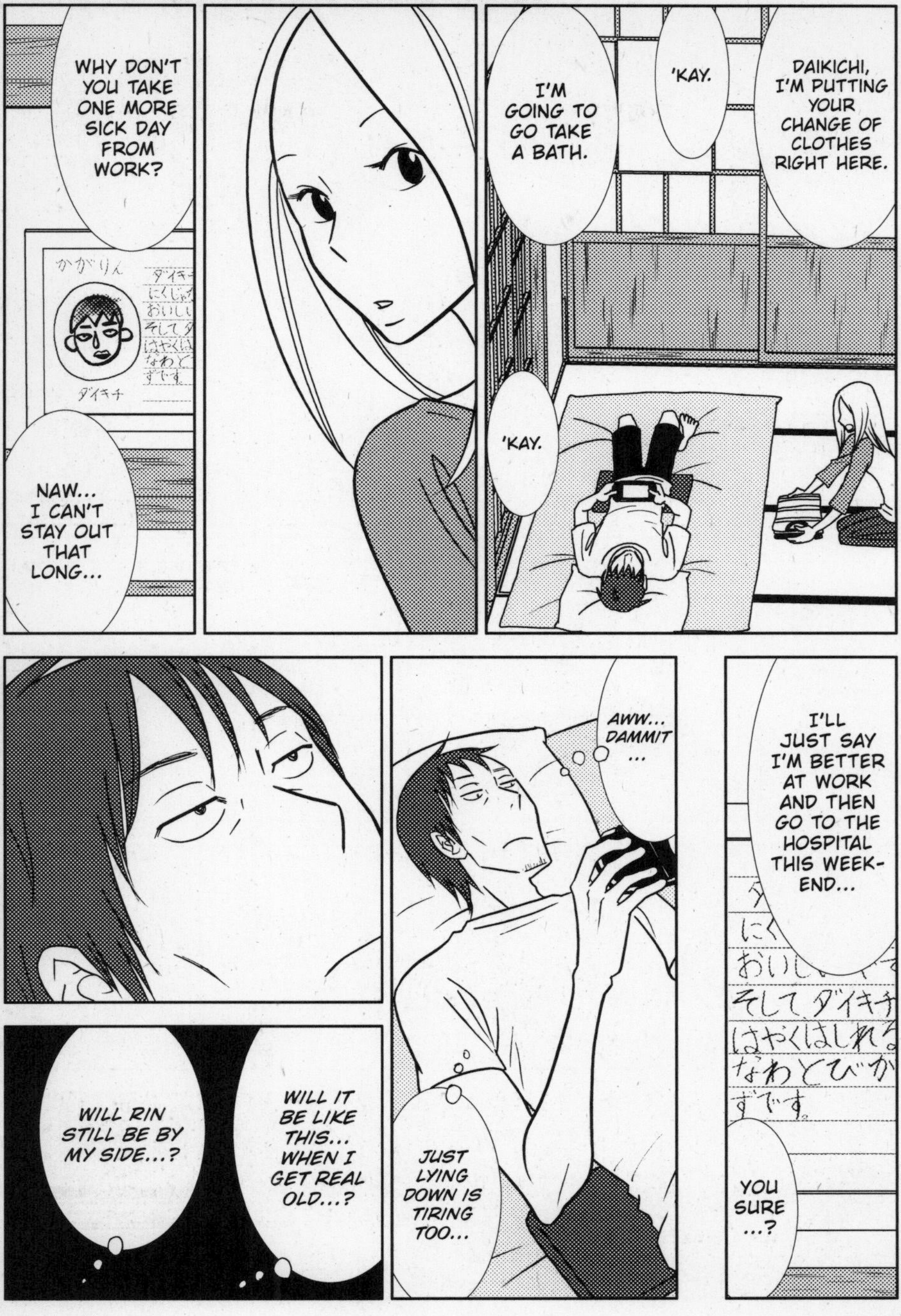

DAIKICHI, I'M PUTTING YOUR CHANGE OF CLOTHES RIGHT HERE.
'KAY.
I'M GOING TO GO TAKE A BATH.
'KAY.
WHY DON'T YOU TAKE ONE MORE SICK DAY FROM WORK?
かがりん
ダイキチ
NAW... I CAN'T STAY OUT THAT LONG...
I'LL JUST SAY I'M BETTER AT WORK AND THEN GO TO THE HOSPITAL THIS WEEK-END...
YOU SURE ...?
AWW... DAMMIT ...
JUST LYING DOWN IS TIRING TOO...
WILL IT BE LIKE THIS... WHEN I GET REAL OLD...?
WILL RIN STILL BE BY MY SIDE...?

NAH... THAT'S NOT RIGHT...
SHE'S SMART...
...AND I WANT HER TO GO AFTER HER OWN DREAMS...
BUT SHE'S TOO NICE...
IF SHE ENDS UP SAYING THAT SHE WANTS TO TAKE CARE OF ME...
...IT'S LIKE... I...

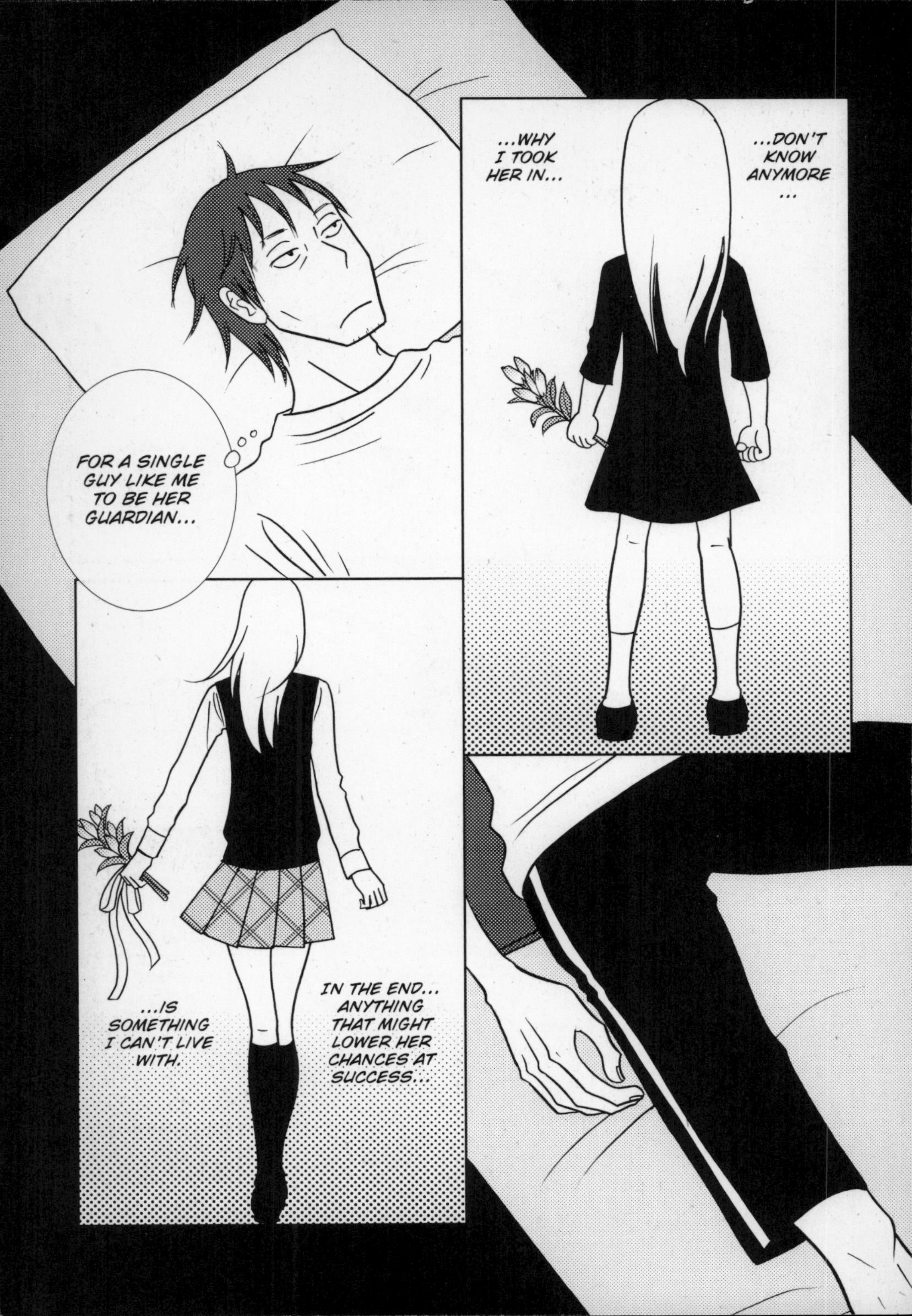

...DON'T KNOW ANYMORE...
...WHY I TOOK HER IN...
FOR A SINGLE GUY LIKE ME TO BE HER GUARDIAN...
IN THE END... ANYTHING THAT MIGHT LOWER HER CHANCES AT SUCCESS...
...IS SOMETHING I CAN'T LIVE WITH.

WOULD IT HAVE BEEN BETTER...
...IF A FAMILY WITH A MOM HAD TAKEN HER?
NOPE...
TOO LATE FOR THAT NOW...
GREAT JOB!
YEAH, REALLY NICE WORK.
SORRY THIS WAS SO RUSHED.
NO PROB-LEM AT ALL.
TO-TALLY.
OH, THE NEXT ONE HAS MORE PAGES, SO SET ASIDE A LITTLE MORE TIME, PLEASE.
GOT IT.

THANK YOU ALL.
SEE YOU ALL AT THE END OF THE MONTH.
NNH ...
GOOD NIGHT.
GOOD-BYE.
SAIONJI-SENSEI, GREAT WORK!!
......
MAA-CHAN IS GOING TO BE A WIFE!
MAA-CHAN, MAA-CHAN ...
...WE'RE ALL DONE WITH THIS JOB, SO LET'S GO TURN IN OUR MARRIAGE REGISTRATION TOMORROW.
STILL !?
EEH!?
LET ME THINK ABOUT IT A LITTLE MORE...

YOU'RE ALREADY SHOWING SO MUCH ...
UM...
...RIN-CHAN'S PROBABLY OUT, BUT...
WAS IT KAWACHI-SAN? WE SHOULD PROBABLY TELL HIM ABOUT YOUR PREGNANCY, RIGHT?
NO WAY!
EHH ...?
I DON'T WANNA GET YELLED AT!
YOU'LL PROBABLY GET YELLED AT MORE IF HE FINDS OUT AFTER THE FACT...
I CAN'T DEAL WITH HIM...
BUT... YOU'RE AN ADULT TOO, MAA-CHAN...

WELL... I DUNNO HOW KAWACHI-SAN WILL FEEL ABOUT THIS, BUT...
...IT'S A COMPLETELY DIFFERENT SET OF CIRCUM-STANCES THIS TIME, RIGHT?
I DON'T WANNA GET LECTURED AT THE AGE OF FORTY...
...AND YOUR FEELINGS MUST BE DIFFERENT THIS TIME AROUND TOO, MAA-CHAN.
IT'S SOME-THING THAT *I*...
...AS A *FATHER*...
...WANT...

UUU...
NGH...
COME ON...
...JUST LIE DOWN FOR NOW...
UGH...
......
DAI-KICHI.
BATH-ROOM?
YEAH...
ふー
PHEW!

WANT TO LEAN ON MY SHOULDER?
I'M FINE.
BUT IT'S TAKING YOU SO LONG...
ずる… ZURU (DRAG)
ZURU ずる…
I SAID, IT'S FINE!!

JUST THE THOUGHT THAT I COULD POSSIBLY CRUSH YOU WHILE YOU'RE SUPPORTING ME...
...IT...
...PAINS ME...
AM I...
...THAT USELESS?
YER PLENTY USEFUL!
BUT YOU LET KOUKI AND THE PEOPLE FROM YOUR JOB HELP YOU...
ヨボ... YOBO (WOBBLE)
PHYSICALLY, THEY'RE COMPLETELY DIFFERENT!!
KOUKI INCLUDED.
OH...
ヨボ... YOBO
ヨボ... YOBO
OF COURSE! I CAN'T LEAN ON A GIRL...
IS THAT IT...?
I'LL HOP IN THE SHOWER TOO SINCE I'M UP ALREADY.

OH...
RIGHT ...
RIN...
SORRY ...
HUH?
PUTTING THIS ON YOU...
...IT'S NOTH-ING.
HEY, WHEN I WAS LITTLE AND STUFF, YOU STAYED WITH ME WHEN I GOT A COLD, RIGHT?
......

I'LL MAKE IT SO YOU WON'T HAVE TO TAKE CARE OF ME WHEN I'M REALLY OLD.
AH HA HA!
WHAT, YOU'RE GOING TO GET A WIFE NOW?
SHUT UP! SHUT UP!
SAME THING WHETHER I GET ONE OR NOT.
DAIKICHI, YOU STILL HAVEN'T LOST HOPE, HUH?
......

WAIT... SO WHEN DAIKICHI CAN'T MOVE ANYMORE ...
...DOES THAT MEAN SOMEONE ELSE WILL...
...TAKE CARE OF HIM ...?
HUH?

I DON'T THINK...
...I LIKE THAT VERY MUCH...
?

BUNNYDROP
episode.39

I'M HOME.
GREAT, YOU'RE BACK.
SORRY I'M LATE.
IT'S OKAY.
HOW'S YOUR BACK ...?
YOU GOT IT LOOKED AT, RIGHT?
YEAH.

A LOT OF CRACKING?
WELL, A LITTLE.
I DON'T KNOW ABOUT THE LONG TERM, BUT...
...I FEEL A LOT BETTER NOW.
I'M REALLY...
...GLAD...
DID Y'KNOW THIS...? THEY TOLD ME IT'S DANGEROUS IF I DON'T SNEEZE LOOKING STRAIGHT AHEAD.
REALLY?
APPARENTLY JUST THE ACT OF SNEEZING PUTS A LOTTA PRESSURE ON THE LOWER BACK.
HUH...

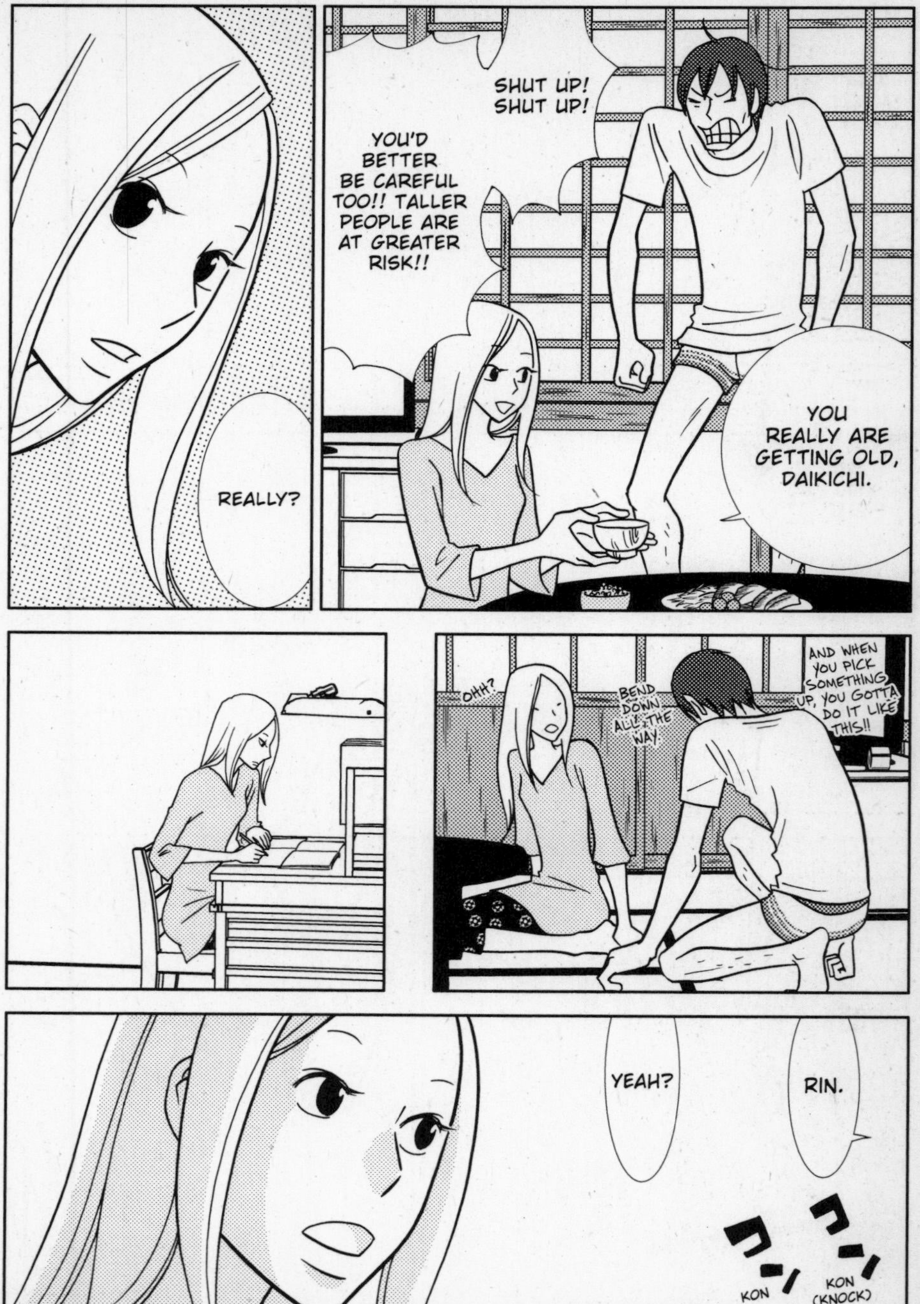

YOU REALLY ARE GETTING OLD, DAIKICHI.
SHUT UP! SHUT UP!
YOU'D BETTER BE CAREFUL TOO!! TALLER PEOPLE ARE AT GREATER RISK!!
REALLY?
AND WHEN YOU PICK SOMETHING UP, YOU GOTTA DO IT LIKE THIS!!
BEND DOWN ALL THE WAY.
OHH?
KON KON (KNOCK)
KON
RIN.
YEAH?

CAN YOU GO THANK KOUKI AND HIS MOM FOR HELPING OUT WITH THIS BACK THING?
MAYBE SATURDAY, TAKE A LITTLE SOMETHING OVER THERE?
SURE.
WHAT SHOULD I TAKE?
I'LL GIVE YOU MONEY, SO...
...JUST GET WHATEVER YOU WANT!!
BUT IT'S SUPPOSED TO BE FROM YOU.
BUCKET: KARAAGE-CHAN
BUT ...
...I ONLY KNOW WHAT KOUKI LIKES!!
からあげちゃん
GENERALLY THE SAME THINGS I LIKE!
DAIKICHI, MAYBE THIS IS WHY YOU'RE NOT MARRIAGE MATERIAL...
I DON'T WANNA HEAR IT!!

OH.
IT'S GRANDMA.
SHE GETS MORE CALLS FROM HER THAN I DO.
HELLO.
IT'S RIN.
GOOD EVENING.
YES, I'M DOING GREAT.
WE'LL COME VISIT AT THE END OF THE YEAR.
DAI-KICHI?
OH, HE THREW OUT HIS BACK RECENTLY...
...BUT HE'S FINE NOW.
OH?
YOU WANT TO TALK TO HIM?
HEY!
DAIKICHI!! GET BACK HERE!!
DOTA (THUD)
DOTA
DOTA

I! TOLD! YOU!!
I'M FINE NOW.
WORK? YEAH, I TOOK SOME SICK DAYS...
BESIDES, MY BACK WON'T GET BETTER JUST 'COS YOU COME, MOM.
NO, IT'S NOT THAT!!
RIN HELPED.
NOT AROUND THE CLOCK!!
I'M HAVING IT LOOKED AT, SO I'M FINE... NO, IT'S NOT LIKE THAT!!
BASHIN (SLAM)
ばしんっ
DON'T TAKE IT OUT ON THE DESK. YOU'RE NOT A KID!
GRR...
I TOLD YOU NOT TO TELL MY MOM.
I THOUGHT IT WOULD BE FINE SINCE YOU WERE BETTER NOW.
YOU'RE SO NAÏVE. DON'T UNDER-ESTIMATE MY MOM.
SHE CAN BE LIKE A DOG WITH A BONE.

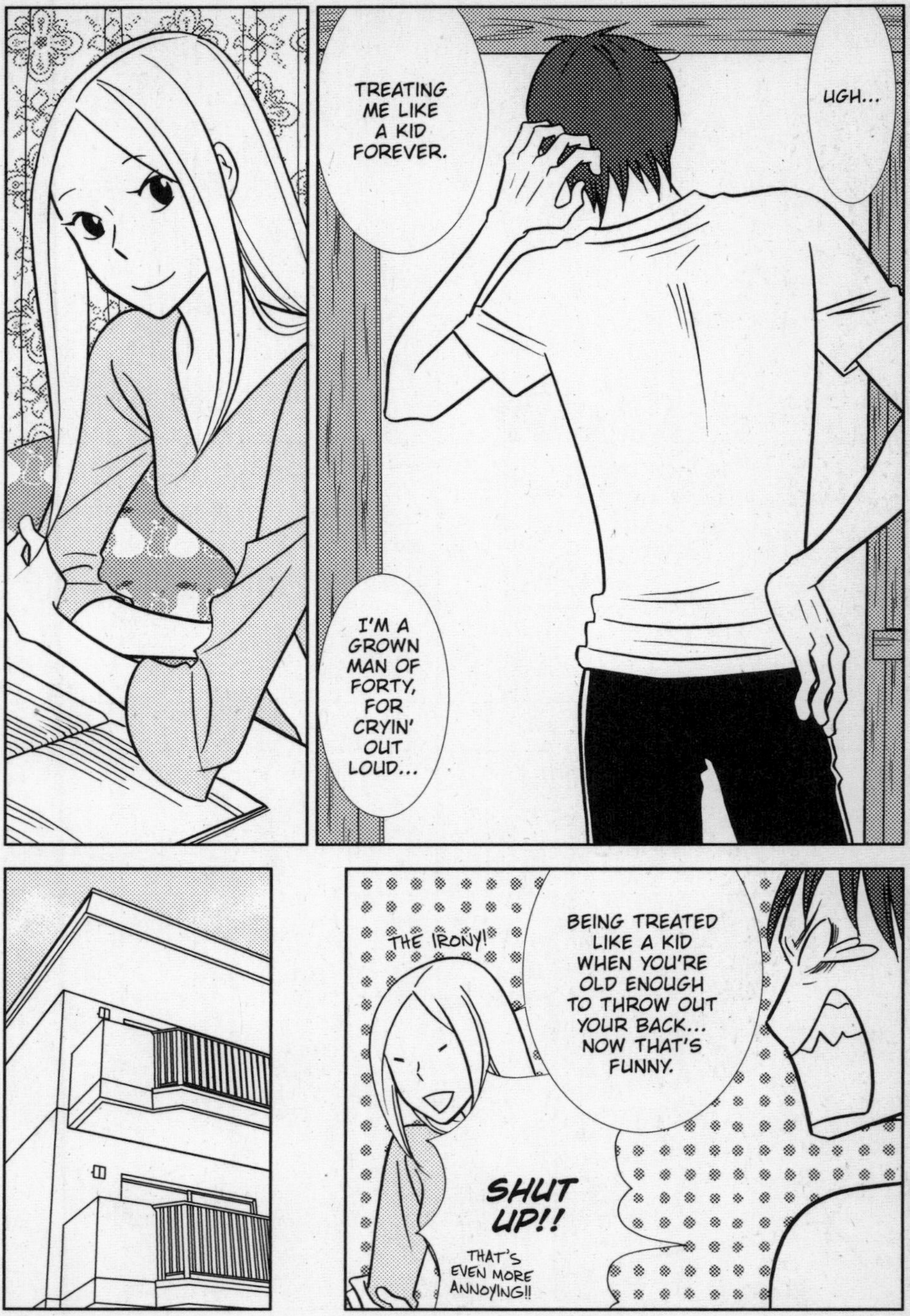
UGH...
TREATING ME LIKE A KID FOREVER.
I'M A GROWN MAN OF FORTY, FOR CRYIN' OUT LOUD...
BEING TREATED LIKE A KID WHEN YOU'RE OLD ENOUGH TO THROW OUT YOUR BACK... NOW THAT'S FUNNY.
THE IRONY!
SHUT UP!!
THAT'S EVEN MORE ANNOYING!!

OH, RIN-CHAN.
HELLO.
HI.
I'M SORRY, KOUKI'S WORKING TODAY.
NO...
I'M HERE TO THANK YOU FOR THE OTHER DAY...
THANK YOU FOR TAKING CARE OF DAIKICHI.
THIS IS JUST A LITTLE SOMETHING...
OH, STOP... I DIDN'T DO ANYTHING...
IS COFFEE ALL RIGHT?
THAT WOULD BE GREAT... THANK YOU.
AH...
CUSTARD PUDDING...

IT WAS A LONG TIME AGO NOW, BUT YOU BROUGHT ME CUSTARD PUDDING BEFORE TOO WHEN I HAD A COLD.
IT MADE ME SO HAPPY.
I THINK IT WAS WHEN YOU WERE IN FIRST GRADE...?
HUH?
REALLY?
THANK YOU.
RIN-CHAN.
I'M SO SORRY... ABOUT KOUKI...
HE'S STILL SUCH A LITTLE BOY...
...ALWAYS CAUSING YOU GRIEF...
NO...
...IT'S OKAY...
WE'RE FRIENDS AGAIN...
...AND I'M FINE WITH IT NOW.

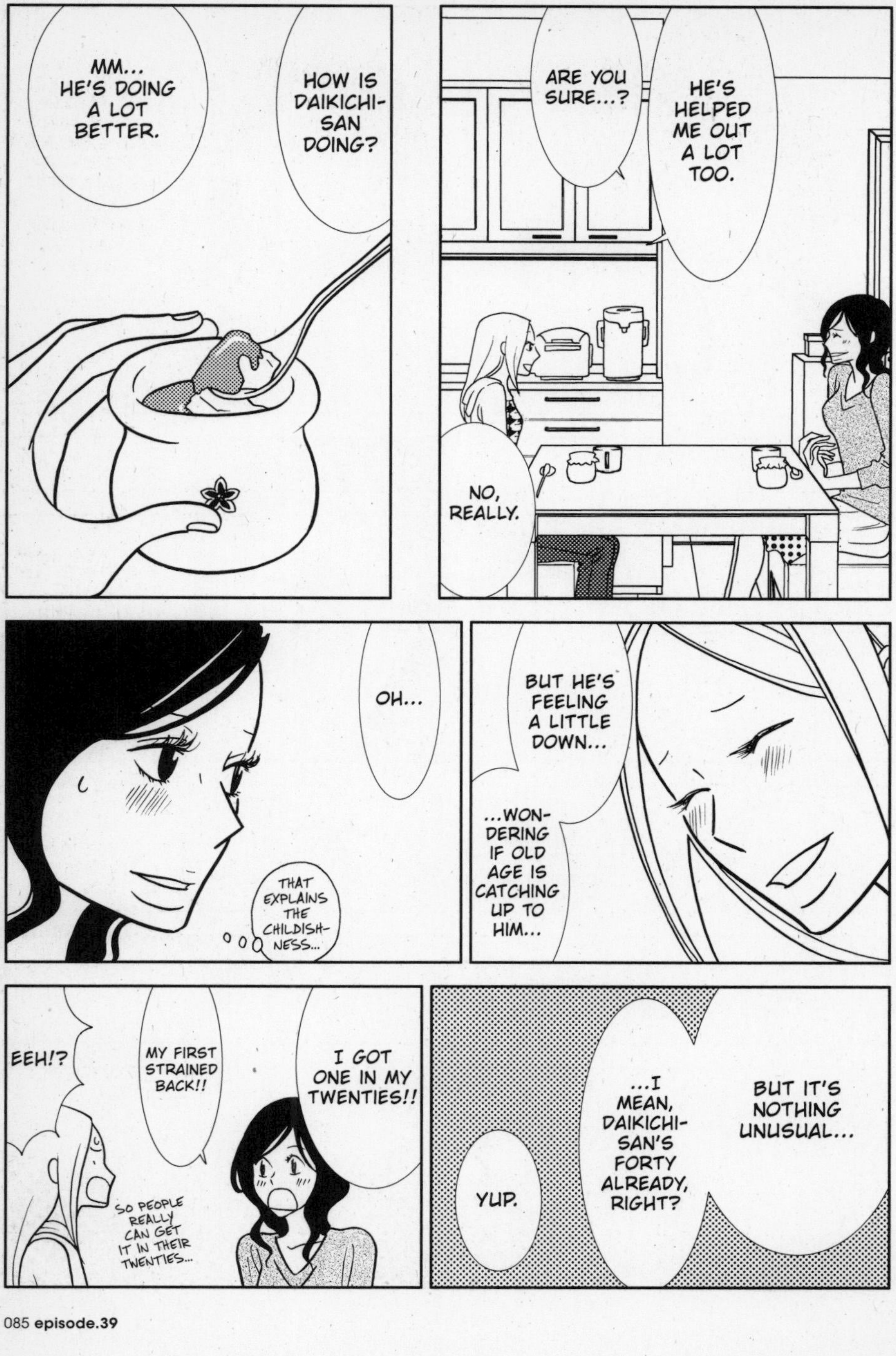

HE'S HELPED ME OUT A LOT TOO.
ARE YOU SURE...?
NO, REALLY.
HOW IS DAIKICHI-SAN DOING?
MM... HE'S DOING A LOT BETTER.
BUT HE'S FEELING A LITTLE DOWN...
...WONDERING IF OLD AGE IS CATCHING UP TO HIM...
OH...
THAT EXPLAINS THE CHILDISHNESS...
BUT IT'S NOTHING UNUSUAL...
...I MEAN, DAIKICHI-SAN'S FORTY ALREADY, RIGHT?
YUP.
I GOT ONE IN MY TWENTIES!!
MY FIRST STRAINED BACK!!
EEH!?
SO PEOPLE REALLY CAN GET IT IN THEIR TWENTIES...

RIGHT... KOUKI, OF COURSE...
HE CONTORTED INTO THESE WEIRD POSITIONS SUDDENLY, SO...
KYAAAAH!
きゃ
I WAS TRYING TO HOLD KOUKI WHILE HE WAS HAVING A PRETTY VIOLENT TANTRUM, AND I GOT THIS EXCRUCIATING PAIN IN MY BACK...
AND JUST WHEN I THOUGHT HE WAS ASLEEP, AND I'D PUT HIM DOWN ON THE FUTON, HE'D START SCREAMING AGAIN...
I WAS ALWAYS HOLDING HIM OR ROCKING HIM...
I GUESS HE HAD SOME SENSORY ISSUES... HE COULDN'T SLEEP WELL, AND EVEN WHEN HE DID, IT WAS A LIGHT SLEEP.
...IN HINDSIGHT, I GUESS IT WAS MY FAULT, FORCING THINGS WHEN I STILL DIDN'T FEEL ALL THAT GREAT RIGHT AFTER GIVING BIRTH.
AND I WAS TIRED TOO, HAVING JUST GONE BACK TO WORK...
PLUS I LEARNED SOME MOVES TO MINIMIZE STRESS ON THE BACK.
BUT AFTER THAT HUMP, I WAS FINE!

I WONDER... IF KOUKI'S DAD WAS BY HER SIDE THEN...
IF... HE WAS ALREADY GONE...HOW HARD IT MUST HAVE BEEN... IT SEEMED HARD EVEN FOR DAIKICHI.
HOW...
...HOW DO YOU DO IT ALL?
PARENTS ARE JUST MADE THAT WAY.
THAT'S HOW WE CAN SOMEHOW RAISE CHILDREN.
KOUKI AND I HAVE BUTTED HEADS PLENTY.
I'VE EVEN SMACKED HIM OVER YOU.
THERE HAVE BEEN TIMES I'VE BEEN REALLY DISAPPOINTED IN MYSELF.
BUT STILL...
...THIS MIGHT NOT BE THE BEST EXAMPLE, BUT...

...EVEN IF KOUKI WERE TO GO WILD AND STRAY FAR OFF THE TYPICAL PATH...
...THE FACT THAT HE'S DEAR TO ME WOULD NEVER CHANGE.
EVER.
SO WHAT I'M DOING, WHAT I HAD TO DO...
...IT'S EASY.
OH...
...THIS IS COMPLETELY IN A DIFFERENT DIMENSION FROM SPOILING HIM OR ANYTHING LIKE THAT.

SO EVEN NOW WHEN HE'S GROWN BIG...
...HE'S STILL CUTE?
OF COURSE.
KOUKI'S SLEEPING FACE NOW AND WHEN HE WAS LITTLE—
SURE, MANY THINGS HAVE CHANGED...
...BUT TO ME, THEY'RE BOTH THE SAME.
HE'S STILL MY SWEET CHILD.

I'M SURE DAIKICHI-SAN FEELS THE SAME WAY...

SHE'S ALWAYS SO NICE...
...BUT SHE'S SO STRONG...
...KOUKI'S MOM.
DAIKICHI SEEMS A LITTLE BIT LIKE A KID IN FRONT OF HIS MOM.
REINA AND HER MOM ARE MORE LIKE SISTERS...
...OR MAYBE FRIENDS...

OH... RIGHT, KAZUMI-ONEECHAN HURT HER BACK ONCE TOO...
SHE DOESN'T SEEM LIKE A "MOM" IN FRONT OF HER OWN MOM EITHER.
SO EVERYONE...
...IS A "SWEET CHILD"?
WHAT IS A "MOTHER," I WONDER...?

HOW AM I REFLECTED IN MY MOTHER'S EYES...?
WHAT'S THIS?
A LITTLE SOME-THING FOR YOU, DAIKICHI.
WHY THE PRESENT ...?

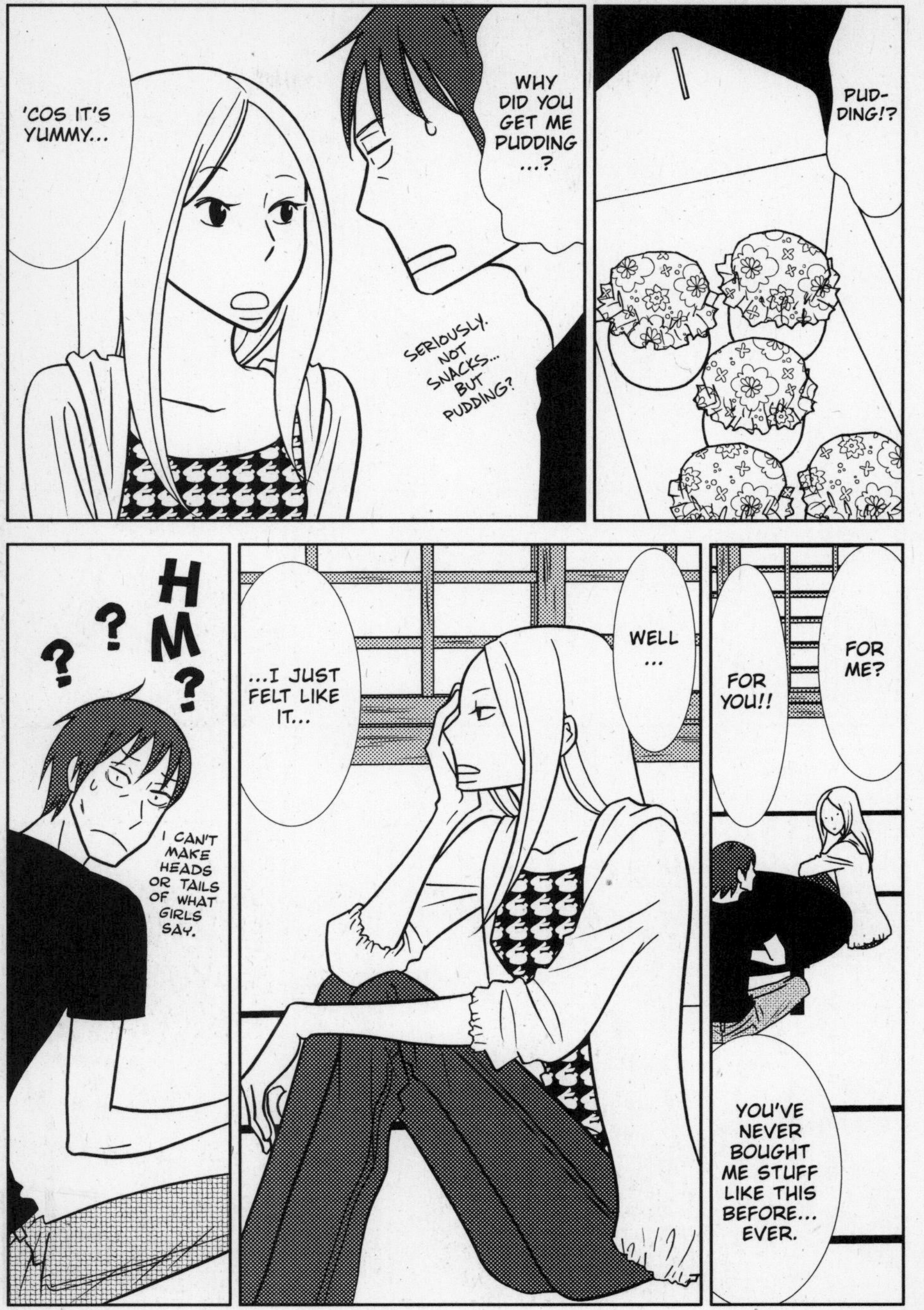
PUD-DING!?
WHY DID YOU GET ME PUDDING ...?
SERIOUSLY. NOT SNACKS... BUT PUDDING?
'COS IT'S YUMMY...
FOR ME?
FOR YOU!!
YOU'VE NEVER BOUGHT ME STUFF LIKE THIS BEFORE... EVER.
WELL ...
...I JUST FELT LIKE IT...
HM?
? ?
I CAN'T MAKE HEADS OR TAILS OF WHAT GIRLS SAY.

SIGN: PUBLIC LIBRARY

BOOKS: FAMILY REGISTRATION LAW / EASY TO UNDERSTAND FAMILY REGISTRATION / FAMILY REGISTRY ENCYCLOPEDIA / EVERYTHING YOU NEED TO KNOW ABOUT FAMILY REGISTRIES / THE LEADER IN FAMILY TREES / MAKE IT!! YOUR FAMILY TREE

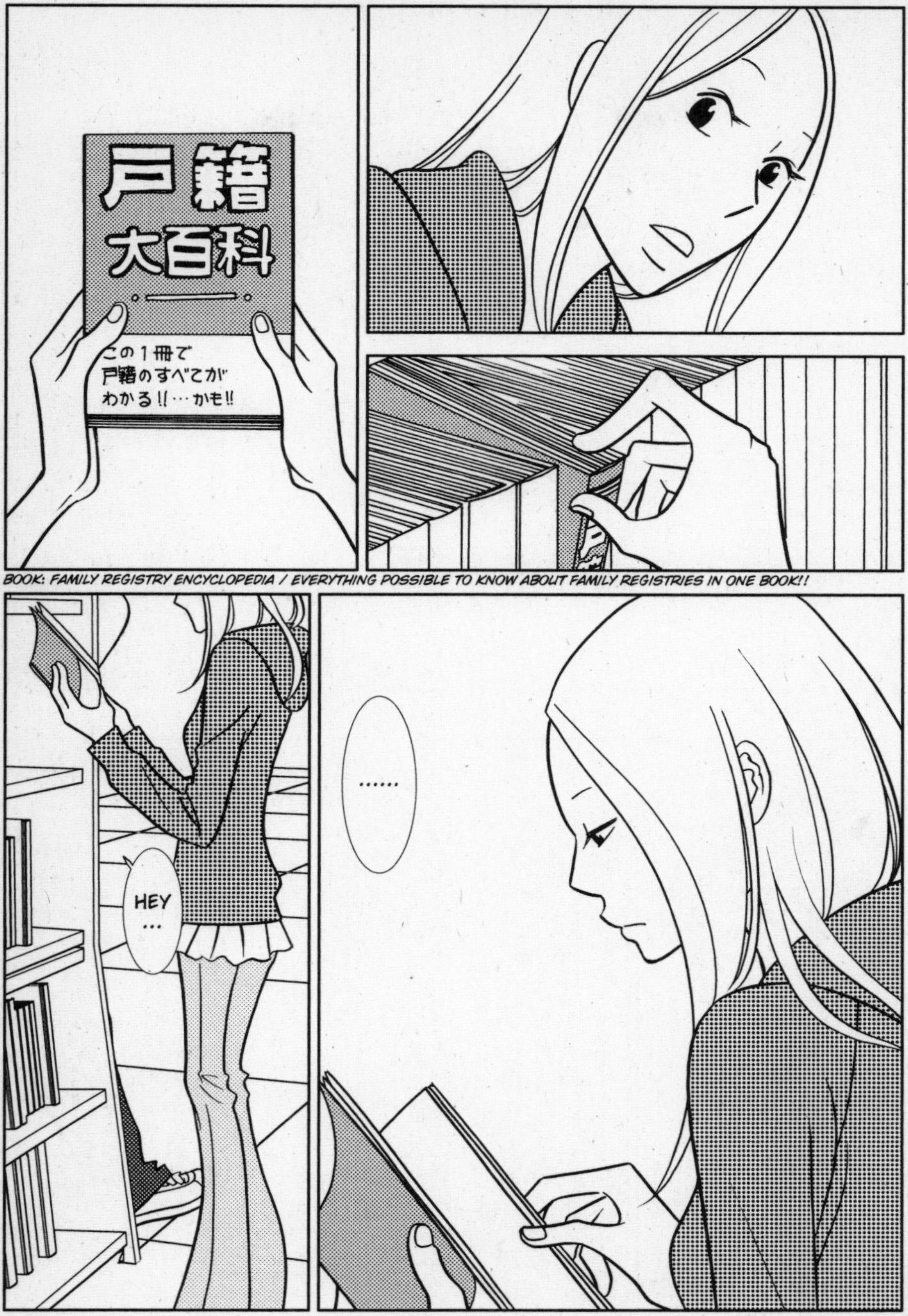
戸籍
大百科
この1冊で
戸籍のすべてが
わかる!!…かも!!
BOOK: FAMILY REGISTRY ENCYCLOPEDIA / EVERYTHING POSSIBLE TO KNOW ABOUT FAMILY REGISTRIES IN ONE BOOK!!
HEY...
……

FAMILY REGISTRY!?
KOUKI...
WHAT THE HECK ARE YOU READING...!?
THAT'S SOME SERIOUS STUFF RIGHT THERE, HUH?
WELL, YOU SEE...
YOU... WANNA MEET YOUR MOM?
HMM...
THAT IS...
...UM, MAYBE NOT...
I DON'T KNOW...

I'M THINKING A LOT ABOUT THE WORD "MOTHER" THESE DAYS...
RIN...?
NOT JUST ABOUT MINE... BUT IN A BROADER SENSE OF THE WORD.
I'M CURIOUS ABOUT WHAT IT MEANS TO BE A "MOTHER"...
AND RIGHT WHEN I WAS THINKING THAT, I SAW THIS BOOK.
SO I WAS JUST LOOKING.
I DIDN'T KNOW ...
...THAT UNDERAGE KIDS CAN SEE THEIR REGISTRIES TOO...
HUH?
I FIGURED... IF I LOOKED AT *THIS*, MY MOM'S NAME WOULD PROBABLY BE ON IT...
......
RIN, DON'T TELL ME...

YEAH...
...I THINK I'LL DIG A LITTLE...
......
YOU GOT GUTS, I'LL GIVE YOU THAT...
DOES THAT MEAN...
...I COULD FIND OUT TOO?
HUH...?
ABOUT YOUR DAD?
YEAH...

AS LONG AS YOU KNOW YOUR REGISTERED RESIDENCE ...
HUH...
YOU WANT TO FIND OUT TOO?
......
NAH...
I THINK I'LL LEAVE IT BURIED...
...MY MOM WOULD GET REAL WORRIED IF SHE FOUND OUT.
BESIDES, I HATE MY DAD.
A *DAD-TYPE PERSON* IS LIKE DAIKICHI. YEAH, DAIKICHI.
WHAT THE HECK?
......

DAIKICHI WOULD WORRY TOO, WOULDN'T HE...?
...I WAS ONLY THINKING ABOUT MYSELF... JUST NOW...
RIN.
HM...?
OUR FAMILY SITUATIONS ARE PRETTY SIMILAR, BUT...
...THE WAY THEY CAME ABOUT ARE COMPLETELY DIFFERENT, RIGHT?
I GUESS...
SO THEN...
...DON'T WORRY ABOUT IT.

IT'S NORMAL TO WONDER ABOUT YOUR OWN MOM, RIGHT?
YOU SHOULD LOOK IT UP IF YOU REALLY WANNA KNOW.
IF...
...BUT IF, ONE DAY...
コト・・・
KOTO (THUNK)

...I WERE TO MEET MY MOM FACE-TO-FACE...
... COULD I...
...STILL STAY IN DAIKICHI'S HOUSE...?
HUH?
IF DAIKICHI HAPPENS TO GET MARRIED SOMEDAY...
...CAN I STILL LIVE WITH HIM...?
RIN, YOU'RE REALLY SMART...
...BUT YOU CAN BE REALLY STUPID, Y'KNOW?
......

WHAT'RE YOU EVEN TALKING ABOUT?
DAIKICHI'S HOUSE IS YOUR HOUSE, RIGHT?
GEEZ... KOUKI...
...I TOLD YOU I CAN DO THIS MYSELF.
STILL!!

SIGN: CITY HALL

BUNNYDROP

BUNNY DROP
episode.40

SIGN: CITY HALL

市民課
OH.
THERE IT IS.
SIGN: CITIZENS' AFFAIRS DIVISION
市民課
市民課
EXCUSE ME.
THIS IS A KOSEKI ...?
KINDA FLIMSY, ISN'T IT?
NO, NO.
THIS IS THE DOCUMENT REQUEST FORM TO GET MY RESIDENT REGISTRY INFORMATION.
HUH? RESIDENT REGISTRY ...?

IF YOU DON'T KNOW YOUR REGISTERED RESIDENCE, THEY WON'T BE ABLE TO GET YOUR KOSEKI.
SINCE I DON'T KNOW MINE.
SO FIRST YOU FIND OUT YOUR REGISTERED ADDRESS THROUGH THE RESIDENT REGISTRY.
HUH...
THAT'S A LOT OF 'EM...
SO YOUR REGISTERED ADDRESS ISN'T THE SAME AS WHERE YOU LIVE?
FORM: NUMBER OF DOCUMENTS / INDICATE FAMILIAL RELATIONSHIP / REGISTERED RESIDENCE / FAMILIAL RELATIONSHIP: INDICATED—
FOR SOME PEOPLE IT'S THE SAME, AND FOR OTHERS IT'S DIFFERENT.
??
〔 通〕
続柄·本籍等を表示します
通〕 続柄 表示する
通〕 本籍 表示する
通〕 使用目的
FORM: REGISTERED RESIDENCE: INDICATED / PURPOSE OF USE—
IN MY CASE, IT'S PROBABLY...
...DAIKICHI'S HOUSE...
...OR GRANDPA'S HOUSE...?

RIN, YOU HAVE A HANKO SEAL?
WE ALL GOT ONE AT OUR MIDDLE SCHOOL GRADUA-ATION CERE-MONY.
WE DID ...?
PAPER: TAKASHI / THIS IS TO CERTIFY— / YEAR
HEY— SO?
NOT YET...I'M GOING TO LOOK NOW...
ONE, TWO...
考
この写しは
平成

OH... MY REGISTERED ADDRESS...
IT'S GRANDPA'S HOUSE...
PAPER: HEAD OF FAMILY - SOUICHI KAGA
筆頭者
鹿賀 宋一
I ONLY LIVED THERE WHEN I WAS REALLY LITTLE.
HUH...
SO I DIDN'T EVEN KNOW MY ADDRESS...

AH!!
WHAT?
EXCUSE ME!! IS MY KOSEKI ONLY AVAILABLE AT MY REGISTERED RESIDENCE?
THAT'S CORRECT.
OH ...
...IS THAT RIGHT ...?
WASN'T YOUR GRANDPA'S PLACE PRETTY FAR AWAY?
GOING THERE AND BACK AFTER SCHOOL WOULD BE...
YEAH... PROBABLY NOT POSSIBLE ...
AND DAIKICHI GETS MAD IF I GET HOME TOO LATE ON A WEEKDAY...
IN THAT CASE, YOU CAN ALWAYS REQUEST IT BY MAIL.
I CAN?
YES.

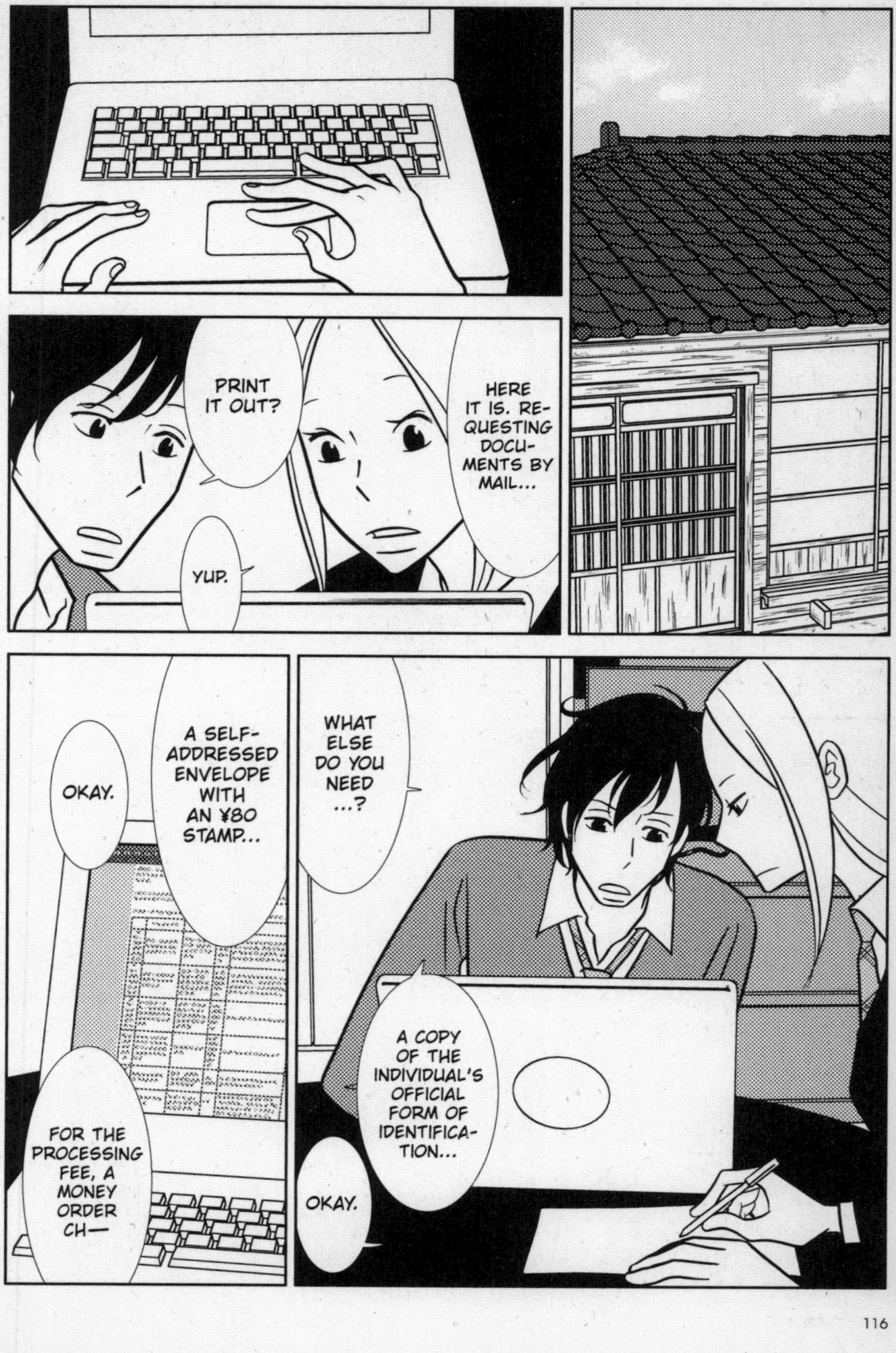
HERE IT IS. REQUESTING DOCUMENTS BY MAIL...
PRINT IT OUT?
YUP.
WHAT ELSE DO YOU NEED...?
A SELF-ADDRESSED ENVELOPE WITH AN ¥80 STAMP...
OKAY.
A COPY OF THE INDIVIDUAL'S OFFICIAL FORM OF IDENTIFICATION...
OKAY.
FOR THE PROCESSING FEE, A MONEY ORDER CH—

...CHE-KWEE?
¥450.
YUP.
FIXED AMOUNT MONEY ORDER CHEQUE.
H-HOW DO YOU KNOW THAT!?
I DON'T KNOW THE DETAILS!!
IT'S A REGULAR ON KANJI TESTS!!
THAT MIS-PRONUNCIATION IS ON TESTS TOO!
SINCE YOU CAN'T SEND ACTUAL MONEY BY MAIL...
...IT'S A POSTAL ORDER IN LIEU OF THAT.
YOU CAN'T SEND CASH BY MAIL?
NO.
HUH...
OKAY! NOW TO JUST STOP BY THE CONVENIENCE STORE AND MAKE A COPY OF MY STUDENT I.D. AND INSURANCE CARD...
...THEN GET THE STAMP AND MONEY ORDER AT THE POST OFFICE...

...AND JUST IN CASE, ERASE THE HISTORY ON THE BROWSER...
WOW. TALK ABOUT THE PERFECT CRIME...
DAIKICHI COUNTER-MEASURE.
SIGN: POST OFFICE
〒
JP
郵便局
AND IT'LL GET THERE JUST LIKE THAT?
YUP.

JUST DON'T LET DAIKICHI FIND OUT.
HE'LL TOTALLY WORRY.
I KNOW.
I'LL BE FINE AS LONG AS I CHECK THE MAIL EVERY DAY AS SOON AS I GET HOME.
I USUALLY GET HOME BEFORE HE DOES...
...SINCE HE'S BEEN WORKING LATE THESE DAYS.
I'M STOPPING BY THE GROCERY STORE NOW TO PICK UP STUFF FOR DINNER.
YOU WANT TO EAT WITH US?
......
I'D REALLY LIKE TO, BUT...

SFX: DAKU (SWEAT) DAKU DAKU

...I DON'T KNOW HOW I'M GONNA ACT NORMAL AROUND DAIKICHI AFTER THIS, SO...
だく だく だく
...I'LL PASS FOR TODAY.
WHAT?
WHAT'S THAT ABOUT?
YOU JUST HAVE TO ACT NORMAL.
YOU HAVEN'T DONE ANYTHING WRONG.
I CAN'T!!
I CAN'T!!
LA-LA-LAAA~

I'M GONNA GO SEE SENPAI FOR A LITTLE BIT.
'KAY.
SORRY, RIN.
IT'S FINE.
SENPAI HAS PRACTICE AFTER SCHOOL, SO IT'S HARD TO SEE EACH OTHER.
I'LL BE BACK SOON.
YUP.

RIN.
DO YOU THINK *IT'LL* GET HERE TODAY?
IT'S NOT THAT FAST.
WE JUST MAILED IT YESTERDAY!

RIGHT!
?
ニヤ NIYA (SMIRK)
ニヤ NIYA
KAGA-SAN.
UM...
WHAT IS IT ...
... TAKE-UCHI-KUN?

IS REINA-CHAN...
...REALLY GOING OUT WITH A SECOND-YEAR?
OH...
UM... MAYBE...
...I THINK...?
...IT'S NOT REALLY CLEAR YET...
OH...
I SEE...
...

BUT ...
...I HAVEN'T HEARD THAT THEY'RE OFFICIALLY DATING YET!!
......
OKAY ...
I UNDERSTAND.
THANKS, KAGA-SAN!
SIGN: KAGA
カタン
KATAN (CLUNK)
河地
NOTHING YET ...
OF COURSE ...
... EVEN BY EXPRESS MAIL, IT'LL BE TOMORROW...
30% OFF

......
YOU KNOW WHAT? KOUKI'S MOM...
HM?
SHE'S PULLED MUSCLES IN HER BACK TOO.

WHAT?
FOR REAL?
WHEN KOUKI WAS A BABY...
OH.
WHEN SHE WAS STILL YOUNG...
I'LL BET KOUKI WAS A WILD CHILD FROM THE MOMENT HE WAS BORN.
I DON'T DOUBT IT...
WELL, I'VE HEARD THE DIFFICULTY OF RAISING TODDLERS IS ON A COMPLETELY DIFFERENT LEVEL...
YOU CAME TO LIVE HERE WHEN YOU WERE SIX, SO I DON'T KNOW ABOUT THAT TIME PERIOD, BUT...
NOT TO MENTION WE'RE TALKING ABOUT KOUKI HERE...

I WONDER IF SHE WAS ALREADY DIVORCED THEN...
I CAN'T ASK THAT!!
I KNOW ...

PAGE: SAMPLE / [DATE OF BIRTH] 10 MAY 1972 / [FATHER] UNITA, FATHER, MALE / [MOTHER] UNITA, MOTHER / [RELATIONSHIP] SECOND DAUGHTER / [DATE OF DELIVERY] 10 MAY / [PLACE OF BIRTH] MIE PREFECTURE / [DATE OF NOTIFICATION] 1972 / [NOTIFIER] FATHER

......
BOOK: FAMILY REGISTRY
KON KON (KNOCK)
RIN?
AH!
Y- YES!
I NEED TO LEAVE A LITTLE EARLIER TOMORROW.
OKAY.
SO DON'T WORRY ABOUT BREAKFAST.
RIGHT.
GOOD NIGHT.
'NIGHT.

IT'S PROLLY GONNA COME TODAY, RIGHT?
HMM...
I DON'T KNOW...
IT MIGHT TAKE LONGER...
REGRET-TING IT?
......

HMM...
IT'S SCARIER...
...THAN I IMAG-INED.
......
HRNNN...
BUT YOU'RE NOT GONNA KNOW THE NAME WRITTEN IN THE SPOT FOR YOUR MOM, SO...
...YOU SHOULDN'T BE BOTHERED BY IT, RIGHT?
!!!

ARE YOU STUPID?
I'M TOTALLY SHOCKED AT THE INSENSITIVITY OF THAT COMMENT!!
UH...
I DIDN'T MEAN...
IT'S JUST... I CAN'T FIND...
...THE RIGHT WORDS ...
...YOU SEEM SO DOWN, SO...
OH!
HOW 'BOUT THIS?
?
IT'S NOT LIKE YOU REALLY NEED TO SEE IT NOW.
SO JUST DON'T LOOK AT ALL!!
WHA—!?
THAT WOULD TAKE GUTS TOO...

HEY, HEY!
RIIIN!
YEAH?
I WANTED TO TALK TO YOU ABOUT SOMETHING ...
DO YOU HAVE TIME TO HANG OUT NOW?
NOW ...?

AH...
WHAT'S UP?
I CAN'T BE TOO LATE GETTING BACK TODAY...
I...
... LIKE, GOT DUMPED...
REINA ...?

IT LOOKS LIKE SENPAI NEVER HAD ANY INTENTION OF DATING ME.
HUH ...?
BUT HE ACTED SO FRIENDLY...
WHAT SENPAI WANTED WASN'T A GIRLFRIEND ...
...BUT A MANAGER FOR THE BASKET-BALL TEAM.
EHH ...?
BUT THAT'S SO...
...THAT'S WHY HE KEPT TALKING ABOUT HIS PRACTICES AND STUFF ALL THE TIME.
WHEN I SAID THAT I WASN'T INTER-ESTED IN BEING A MAN-AGER...
...HE GOT ALL... DISTANT ...

THAT JUST MAKES ME MAD.
WELL, WHEN IT'S THIS CUT-AND-DRIED...
AH HA HA!
...YOU CAN ONLY LAUGH ABOUT IT, RIGHT...?
BUT SERIOUSLY...
...IF THAT WAS HOW IT WAS GONNA BE, DON'T KISS ME...YOU KNOW?
I...
GUESS I WAS IN MY OWN FANTASY LAND...
...I FEEL LIKE SUCH AN IDIOT...
REINA...

WANNA GO GET SOMETHING TO EAT?
SOME-THING...
...SWEET...
...AND YUMMY!
YEAH!!
YOU'RE JUST TOO POPULAR, REINA...
I'M JUST LUCKY AS LONG AS I DON'T GET CAUGHT BY ANY STUPID GUYS...
AH HA HA!

SIGN: KAWACHI
河地
カタ
KATA (CLACK)
OH NO...
DAI-KICHI'S ALREADY HOME!!

NOTH-ING AGAIN...
DID DAIKICHI...?
BUT IT'S ONLY BEEN TWO DAYS...
...STILL TOO SOON, I BET...
I'M HOME.
HEY, GOOD, YOU'RE BACK.
DAIKICHI, SORRY. YOU'RE HOME E-EARLY...
I'LL MAKE DINNER NOW...
......
YEAH, WELL, I CAN MAKE DINNER MYSELF, SO THAT'S FINE, BUT...
WH—
WHAT...?

AT LEAST COME BACK HOME BEFORE IT GETS DARK!!
HUH ...?
TH-THAT'S IMPOSSIBLE...
IT'S FALL GOING INTO WINTER... WHAT TIME WOULD I NEED TO LEAVE SCHOOL TO GET HOME WHILE IT'S STILL LIGHT OUT...?
THAT'S WHAT HE'S MAD ABOUT !?
BUT THE KIDS GOING TO AFTER-SCHOOL CLASSES GET HOME AT NIGHT ...
YOU'RE NOT OTHER KIDS!!
AND YOU DON'T GO TO AFTER-SCHOOL CLASSES.
THEN HOW WAS IT WHEN YOU WERE IN HIGH SCHOOL?
YOU'RE NOT ME!!
WHAT IS WITH YOU ...?
I'M GETTING CHANGED ...
RIN...

鹿賀りん様
...THIS IS YOUR HANDWRITING, RIGHT?
WHAT WERE YOU DOING AT A GOVERNMENT OFFICE?
ENVELOPE: TO MISS RIN KAGA
!!!
THE PEOPLE AT CITY HALL...
THEY'RE QUICK ...!!

BUNNY DROP
episode.41

BUNNY**DROP**

WHAT KINDA DOCUMENTS DOES A YOUNG GIRL OF SIXTEEN NEED FROM CITY HALL?
WHAT'S IN HERE?
......

KO...
KOSEKI ...

Y—
YOURS ...?
......
Y... ES...

OH...
RIGHT ...
I GET IT...
YOU WERE TRYING ...
...TO FIND OUT ABOUT YOUR MOM?
......
コク
KOKU (NOD)

HM...
OH, BUT IT'S NOT LIKE I'VE BEEN THINKING ABOUT THIS FOREVER, OKAY?
IT'S LIKE... I DON'T REALLY KNOW MUCH ABOUT MY MOTHER...
BUT THEN CERTAIN THINGS HAPPENED, AND IT JUST STARTED TO WEIGH ON MY MIND...
...THEN BEFORE I KNEW IT... I COULDN'T STOP...
I DON'T EVEN KNOW MY-SELF...
...HOW BAD I WANT TO KNOW...
YEAH...
DAIKICHI...
YOU'RE NOT MAD...?
MAYBE IT'S JUST THAT TIME IN YOUR LIFE...
......

RIN, YOU HAVE A RIGHT TO KNOW.
IT'S NOT SOMETHING I'D GET MAD ABOUT.
DAIKICHI ...
BUT...
...IF YOU STEP INTO THIS BLINDLY...
...THERE'S A BIG CHANCE THAT YOU MIGHT GET HURT. JUST KNOW THAT.

THAT'S WHY, TRUTHFULLY...
...THERE ARE CERTAIN THINGS THAT I WANT YOU TO LET ME CONTROL.
SO...
...AFTER CONSIDERING THE POSSIBILITY OF GETTING HURT...
...YOU STILL WANNA MEET HER?
YOU WANNA MEET YOUR MOM?

YES.

RIN...
DID IT COME?
YEAH.
WHAAA!? FOR REAL?
W-WELL?
ACTU-ALLY...
...DAIKICHI GOT TO THE ENVELOPE FIRST.

AND NOW WE'RE GOING TO GO SEE MY MOM THIS WEEKEND.
SO I DIDN'T GET TO SEE WHAT WAS INSIDE.
DAIKICHI TOOK IT.
EEEEH ...!?
WHY? WHY?
YOU'RE GONNA SEE HER?
YOU OKAY WITH THAT, RIN?
I GUESS.
'COS!
EVEN IF I HEARD ABOUT THIS PERSON FROM DAIKICHI...
...IN THE END, IT'S ALL ABOUT A ***STRANGER*** TO ME.
MAYBE HE FIGURES IT WOULD BE EASIER TO JUST LET US MEET?
......

D—
D'YOU WANT ME TO GO WITH YOU?
DAIKICHI SAID HE'D COME WITH ME.
OH... RIGHT...
RIGHT...
TIME-TABLE?
YEAH...

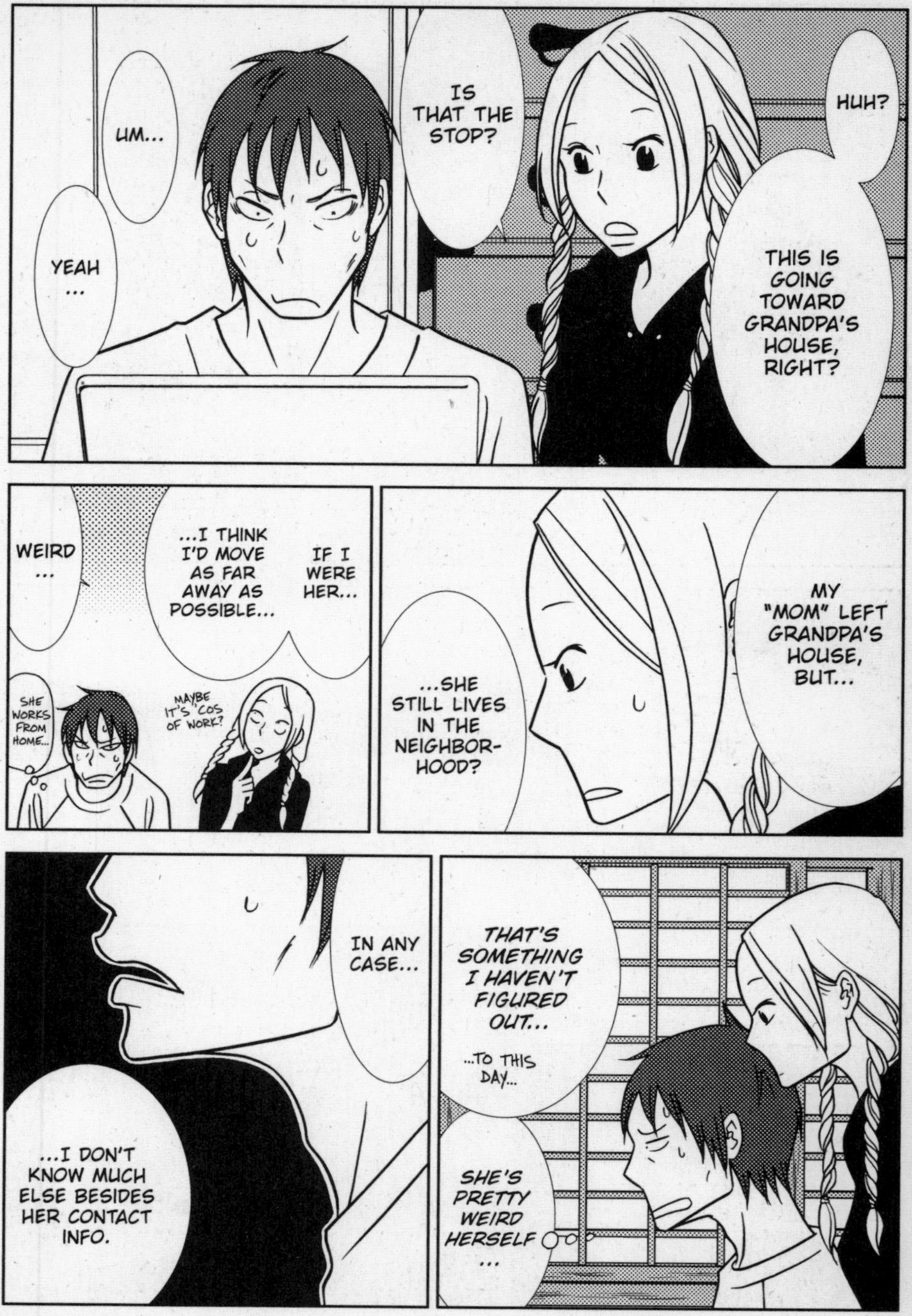
HUH?
THIS IS GOING TOWARD GRANDPA'S HOUSE, RIGHT?
IS THAT THE STOP?
UM...
YEAH...
MY "MOM" LEFT GRANDPA'S HOUSE, BUT...
...SHE STILL LIVES IN THE NEIGHBOR-HOOD?
IF I WERE HER...
...I THINK I'D MOVE AS FAR AWAY AS POSSIBLE...
WEIRD...
MAYBE IT'S 'COS OF WORK?
SHE WORKS FROM HOME...
THAT'S SOMETHING I HAVEN'T FIGURED OUT...
...TO THIS DAY...
SHE'S PRETTY WEIRD HERSELF...
IN ANY CASE...
...I DON'T KNOW MUCH ELSE BESIDES HER CONTACT INFO.

......
......
IF YOU'LL FEEL BETTER MEETING HER, THEN DO IT.
THAT'S ALL.
RIGHT.
YOU DON'T HAVE TO DO THIS NOW...
I KNOW ...
IF YOU DON'T WANNA GO TO YOUR MOM'S PLACE, YOU CAN CALL THIS OFF AT ANY TIME, OKAY?
'KAY ...

ペタ
PETA
ペタ
PETA (PAT)
HMM ...
WHAT?
CAN'T SLEEP?
FEELING A LITTLE NERVOUS ...
I SEE ...

SO DAIKICHI, YOU DON'T KNOW ANYTHING ABOUT MY MOM?
HRRN... NOT MUCH.
WE KEEP IN TOUCH JUST IN CASE SOMETHING HAPPENS.
WE'VE ONLY EVER TALKED A LITTLE BIT.
I WONDER WHAT KIND OF PERSON SHE IS ...?
HMM... DUNNO.
ONE THING, THOUGH... I FEEL BAD SAYING THIS 'COS SHE'S YOUR MOM AND ALL, BUT...
...I JUST CAN'T GET TO LIKE HER.
......

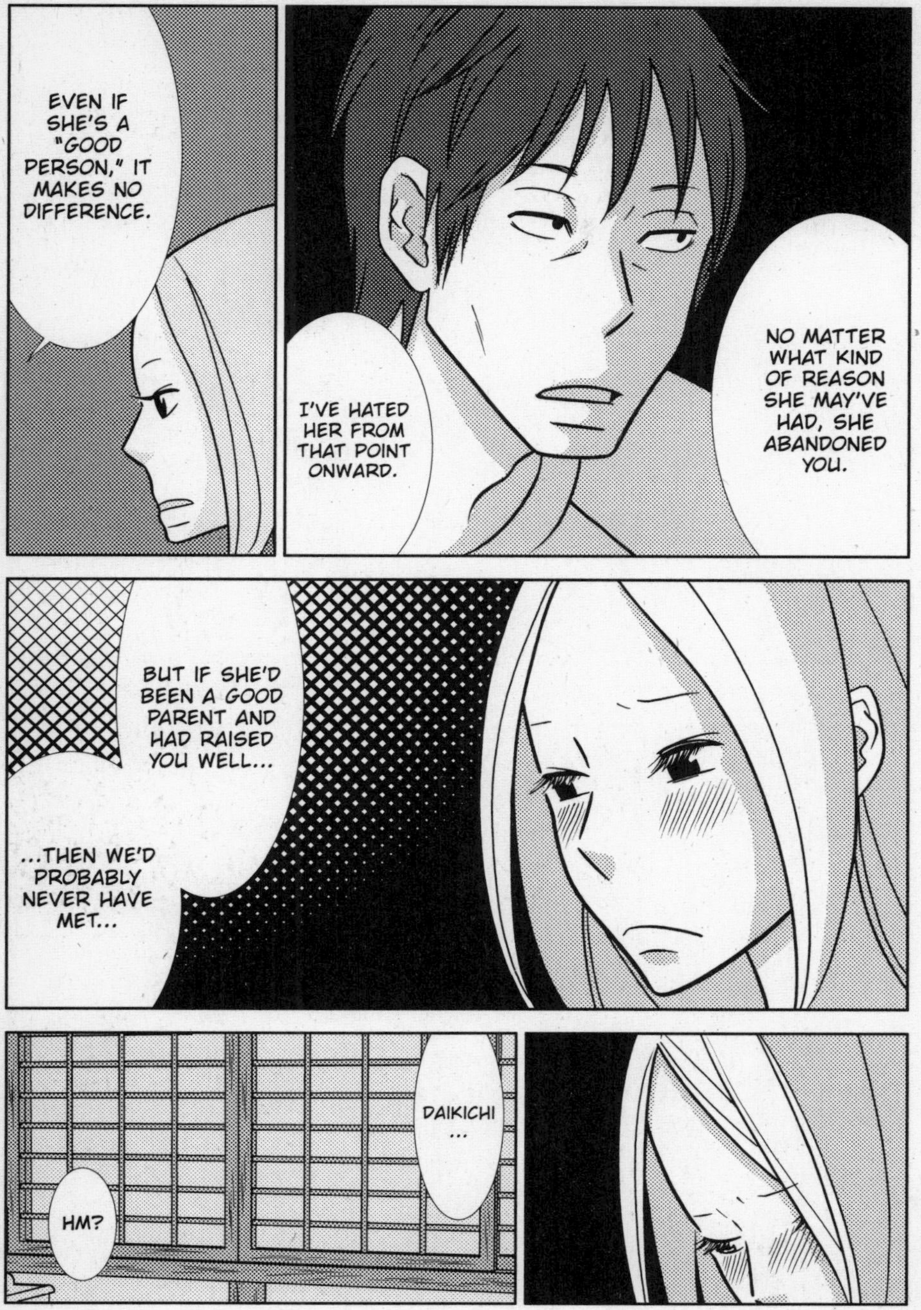
NO MATTER WHAT KIND OF REASON SHE MAY'VE HAD, SHE ABANDONED YOU.
I'VE HATED HER FROM THAT POINT ONWARD.
EVEN IF SHE'S A "GOOD PERSON," IT MAKES NO DIFFERENCE.
BUT IF SHE'D BEEN A GOOD PARENT AND HAD RAISED YOU WELL...
...THEN WE'D PROBABLY NEVER HAVE MET...
DAIKICHI ...
HM?

EVEN AFTER I MEET MY MOM...
...CAN I STILL BE A CHILD IN YOUR HOUSE?
OF COURSE.
YOU'LL BE MY KID FOREVER.

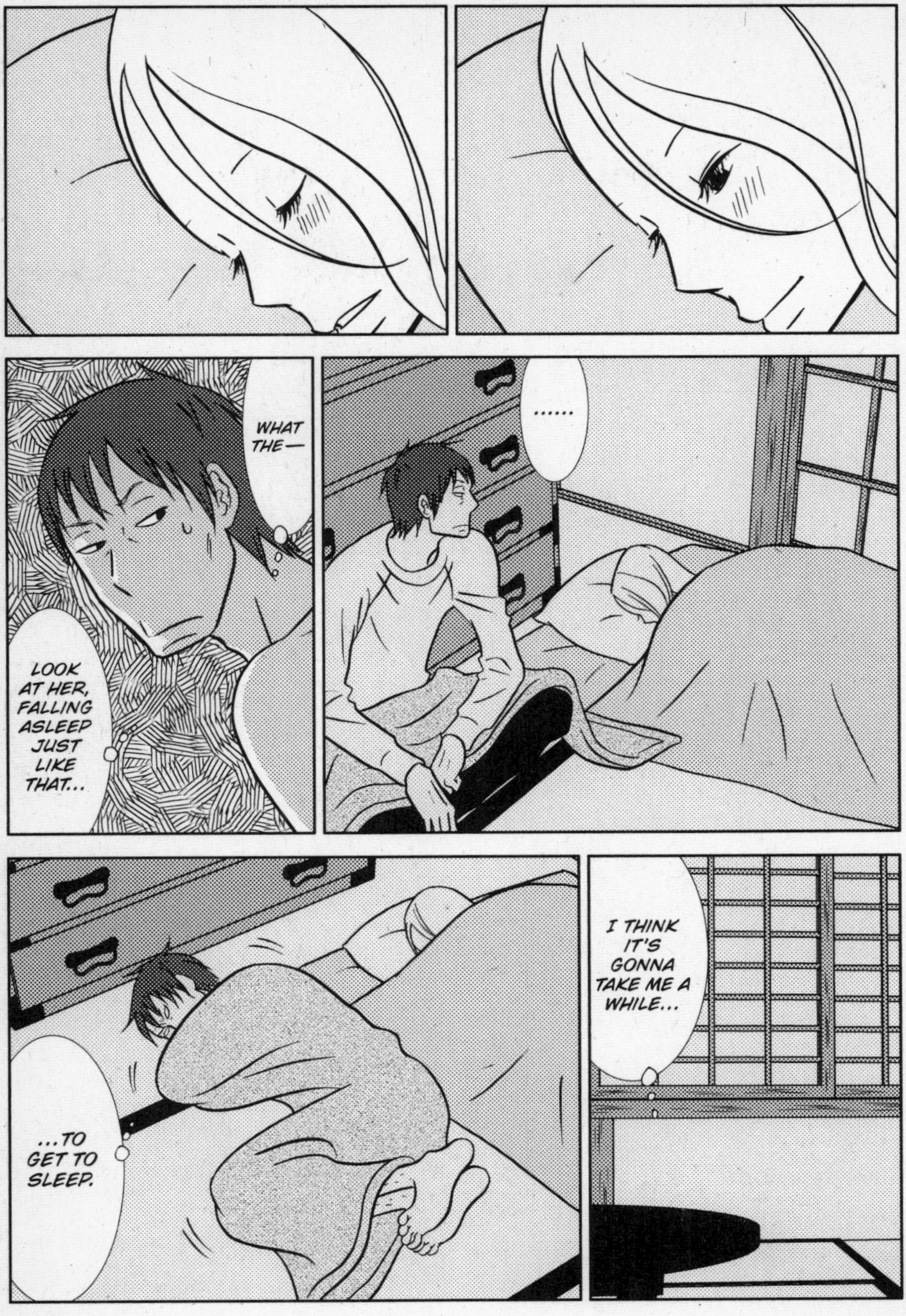
WHAT THE—
LOOK AT HER, FALLING ASLEEP JUST LIKE THAT...
......
I THINK IT'S GONNA TAKE ME A WHILE...
...TO GET TO SLEEP.

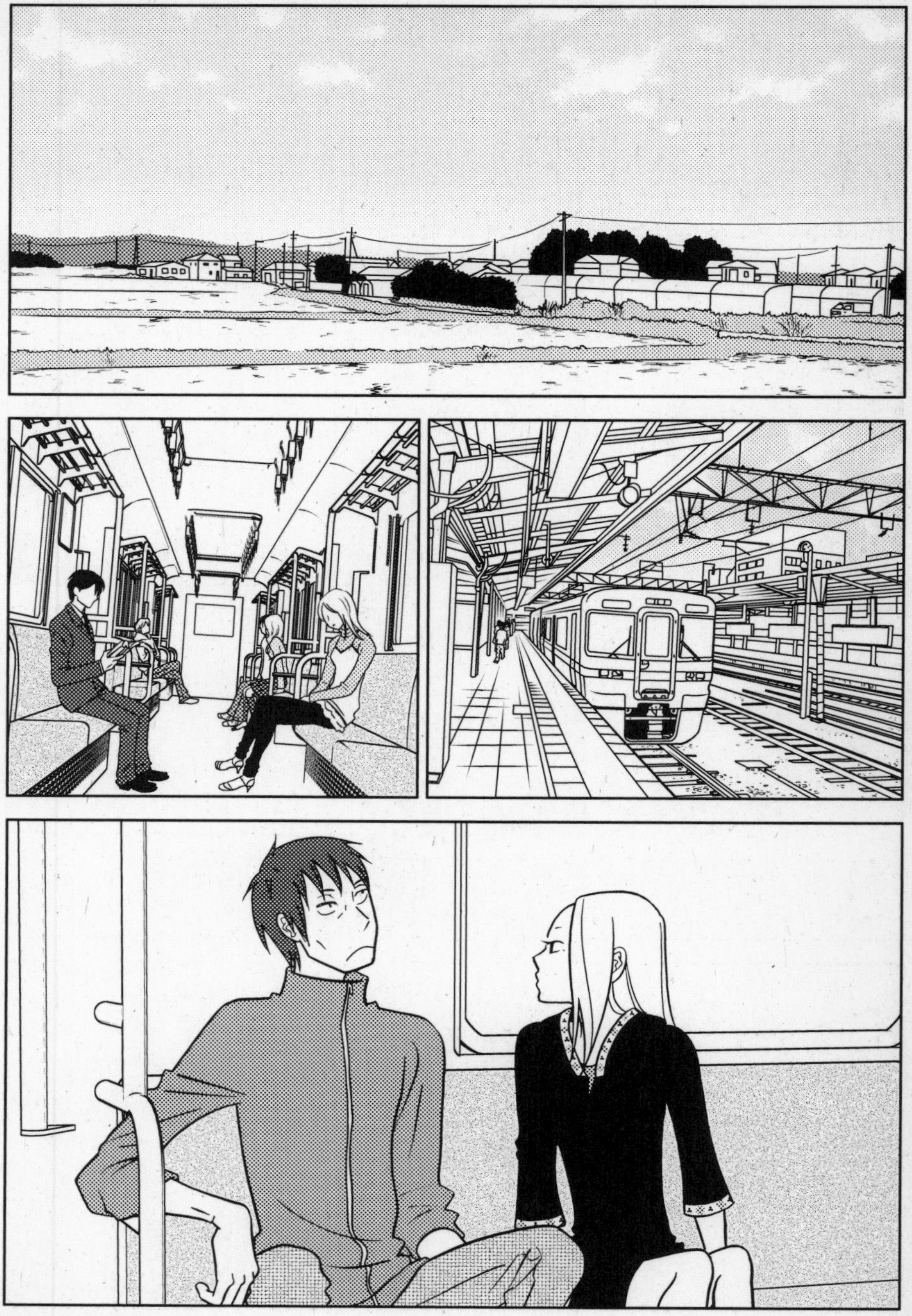

STILL ...
...YOU GETTING THE KOSEKI BY YOURSELF, RIN...
IT MADE ME FEEL A LITTLE LONELY.
I KNOW IT MUST'VE BEEN TOUGH TO TALK ABOUT, BUT STILL.
WELL ...
...YOU KNOW, PUBERTY!
DON'T SAY IT LIKE THAT...
I JUST THOUGHT YOU'D WORRY...
ARE YOU ...
...A TOTAL IDIOT !?

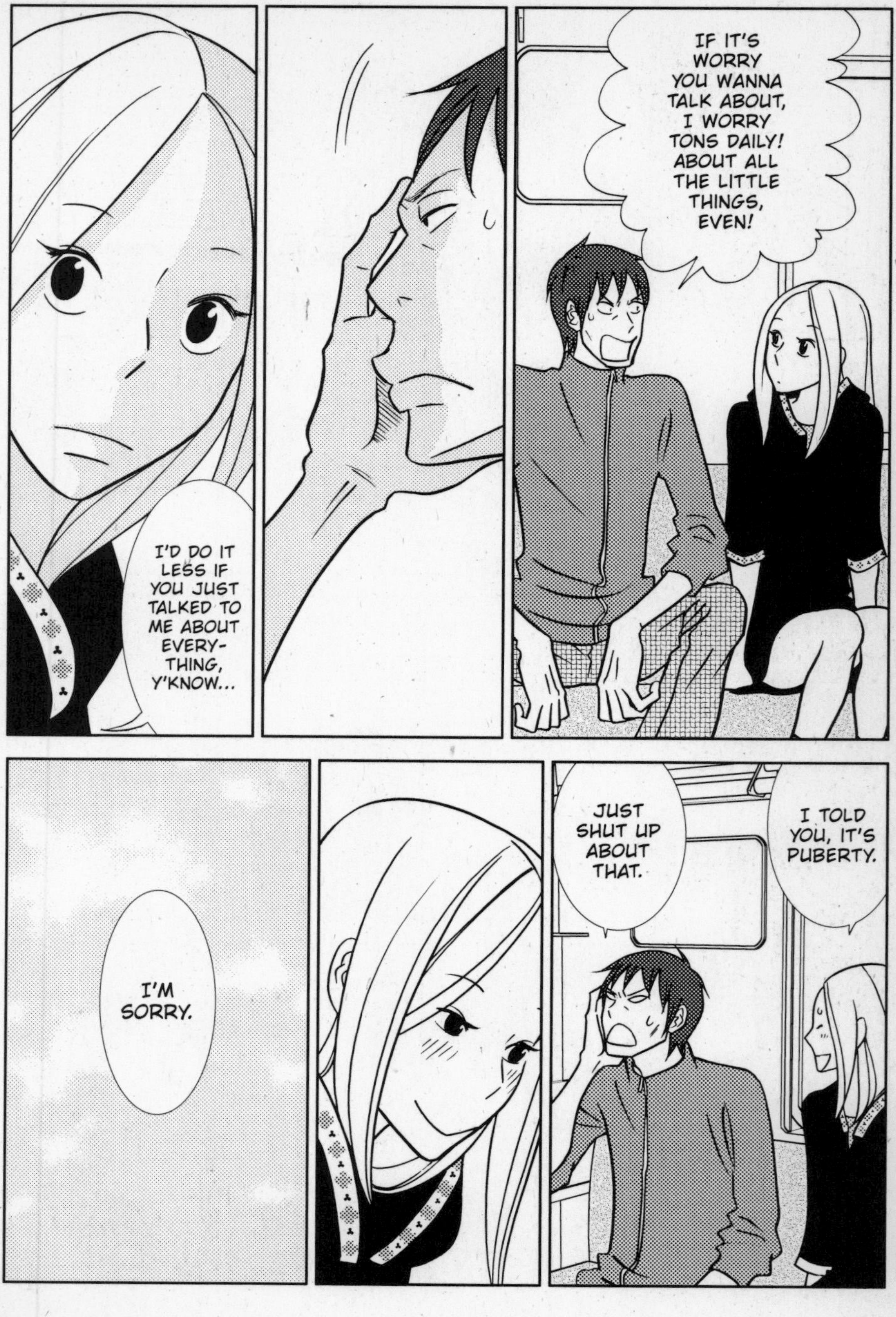
IF IT'S WORRY YOU WANNA TALK ABOUT, I WORRY TONS DAILY! ABOUT ALL THE LITTLE THINGS, EVEN!
I'D DO IT LESS IF YOU JUST TALKED TO ME ABOUT EVERY-THING, Y'KNOW...
I TOLD YOU, IT'S PUBERTY.
JUST SHUT UP ABOUT THAT.
I'M SORRY.

What?
Me? Meet her?
Wha— B-but...that's impossible... It's so sudden...
And... actually I'm gonna be thumbing this week...
THUMBING??
SO YOU'RE SAYING YOU'RE BUSY THIS WEEK?
Yes.
THEN HOW 'BOUT NEXT WEEK?
Next week'll be crazy with drawing.
CRAZY WITH DRAWING??
THEN THE WEEK A-AFTER THAT?
Th-the week after that will be thumbing the next install-ment.

THEN WHEN AREN'T YA BUSY!?
WHAT THE HELL DOES SHE MEAN BY THUMBING!?
Please go through my editors.
HOW CAN I ASK THEM FOR SOMETHING LIKE THIS!?
I MEAN, YER OWN DAUGHTER'S ASKIN' TO SEE YOU!
I'M JUST ASKIN' YOU TO SPARE TWENTY, NO, TEN MINUTES OF YOUR TIME!!!
!!!
ARE YOU THREATEN-ING ME!?
THREAT-ENING!?
YOU'RE A JERK!!
H-HEY...
HUH? MAA-CHAN?

THAT'S NOT IT...
AAGH ...
THIS IS TIRING ...
HENAAA (SLUMP)
AWW... I CAN'T TAKE MUCH MORE OF THIS...
THE DAUGHTER YOU ABANDONED IS ASKING TO SEE YOU.
ISN'T IT REASONABLE FOR YOU, AS THE PARENT, TO SEE YOUR CHILD?
I JUST CAN'T STAND HER...
SFX: HARA (PANIC) HARA
ARE YOU OKAY? THIS ISN'T CAUSING PRENATAL STRESS, IS IT?
......
ALSO ...
...REST ASSURED ...
...AS YOU REQUESTED, Rin will continue to be my child.
......

Fine.
I'll try to carve out some time.
WHY'S SHE GOTTA SAY IT LIKE THAT JUST TO PISS ME OFF...?
YES... IF YOU COULD ...
AND ALSO ...
...I'D LIKE TO ASK YOU TO...
ピ!
PI (BEEP)
GRRRRR!!
AAAGH ...!!
ガチャーン
GACHAAAN (CRASH)
ガシャーン
GASHAAAN (SMASH)
ばっさ
BASSA (FWAP)
ばっさ
BASSA
CAN'T BELIEVE... STUPID!!
WHY DOES HE ALWAYS HAVE TO BE SO —?
STUPID!!
HEY, STOP... I'M THE ONE WHO HAS TO CLEAN UP.
I HATE HIM!!
AND YOU'RE BOTHERING THE NEIGHBORS...
THE WAY HE PUTS THINGS ALWAYS TICKS ME OFF!!
HATE HIM!!

WHAT?
YOU'RE GOING TO MEET RIN-CHAN THIS WEEK!?
EEEEEEH?
YUP ...
BUT MAA-CHAN, YOU SAID THAT YOU DIDN'T WANT TO TELL KAWACHI-SAN ABOUT YOUR PREGNANCY...
I GAVE HIM A CONDITION. WHEN WE MEET, IT'LL JUST BE HER...
OH...
BUT WHEN RIN-CHAN TELLS KAWACHI-SAN LATER, HE'LL FIND OUT, WON'T HE?

EVEN A JERK LIKE HIM WOULDN'T COME BY LATER OR CALL...
...TO YELL AT A PREGNANT LADY WHO'S ABOUT TO POP.
MAA-CHAN ...?
I DON'T CARE IF HE FINDS OUT AFTER THE FACT.
WOW.
YOU GOT A BAD-GIRL PREGNANT LADY THING GOING ON, HUH...?
YOU'RE REALLY TAKING ADVANTAGE OF BEING PREGNANT...

BESIDES, MY WORK WON'T GET DONE IF I LET MYSELF GET DISTRACTED WITH STUFF LIKE THIS.
......
BUT MAA-CHAN...
...THE ONE YOU REALLY NEED TO WORRY ABOUT...
...ISN'T THIS KAWACHI-SAN...
...BUT RIN-CHAN, AND WHAT SHE'S GOING TO THINK ONCE SHE SEES YOUR BELLY.
RIGHT?

DAMMIT! EVERYONE JUST SHUT UP!!
IF I LET MYSELF BE BOTHERED BY THAT ON TOP OF EVERYTHING ELSE...
...I WOULD NEVER GET A LICK OF WORK DONE AT ALL!!
SHUT UP!!
SHUT UP!!
JUST LEAVE ME ALONE!!
NO MORE LECTURES!!
IT'S NOT MY FAULT!!
I DIDN'T DO ANY-THING WRONG!
THE REASON FOR THIS BELLY IS YOU!!
IT'S NOT MY FAULT!!
NOT MYYYY FAULT!!
I HAVE TO FORCE MYSELF TO THINK THAT...
...OR ELSE...

...I CAN'T MOVE FORWARD.
EVER SINCE RIN WAS IN MY BELLY SEVENTEEN YEARS AGO...
...THAT'S HOW IT'S ALWAYS BEEN.
AND PROBABLY HOW IT ALWAYS WILL BE FROM NOW ON...
OH...
IS IT THE NEXT STOP?
YUP...
YOU SURE YOU'RE OKAY GOING ALONE?

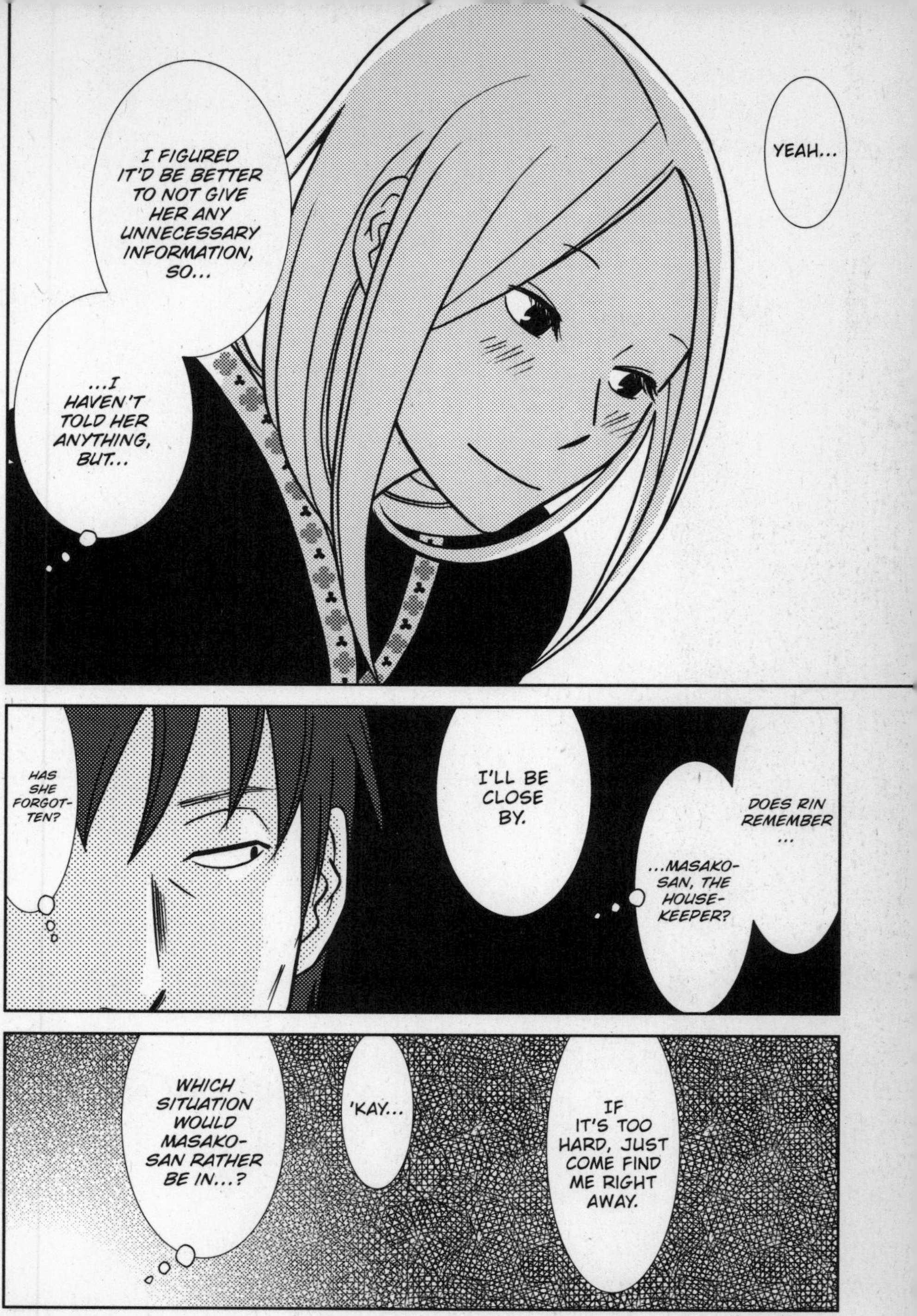
YEAH...
I FIGURED IT'D BE BETTER TO NOT GIVE HER ANY UNNECESSARY INFORMATION, SO...
...I HAVEN'T TOLD HER ANYTHING, BUT...
DOES RIN REMEMBER...
...MASAKO-SAN, THE HOUSE-KEEPER?
I'LL BE CLOSE BY.
HAS SHE FORGOT-TEN?
IF IT'S TOO HARD, JUST COME FIND ME RIGHT AWAY.
'KAY...
WHICH SITUATION WOULD MASAKO-SAN RATHER BE IN...?

BUNNYDROP
episode.42

BUNNY**DROP**

SO I'LL BE WAITING AT THE RESTAURANT WE WERE JUST AT.
RIGHT.
THIS IS THE APART-MENT NUMBER. YOU'LL BE OKAY?
YUP.
I'LL BE GOING THEN...
OKAY.
PAPER: MASAKO YOSHII
RIN.

YOU'LL ALWAYS BE MY KID!!
DON'T YOU WORRY ABOUT THAT!!

I WONDER WHAT KIND OF PERSON SHE IS...
...MY "MOTHER" ...
YES?
GACHA (CLACK)
IT'S RIN.
PLEASE, COME ON IN.
THANK YOU.

WOW ...
IT'S LIKE YOU LOOK ALIKE...BUT NOT ALIKE AT ALL...
......
YOU'RE REALLY TALL.
HOW TALL?
5'6"...
WE'RE ABOUT THE SAME, THEN...
HA HA!

WELL, C'MON IN...
IT'S CRAMPED, BUT...

BOOKS ...
COMPUTER ...
I WONDER WHAT THAT BOX IS FOR ...?
IS HE HER HUSBAND?
HER BELLY ...
I'M SORRY... IT'S KIND OF...
I HAVE ALMOST TOO MUCH TO ASK...
OF COURSE. NO NEED TO FEEL RUSHED ...
DON'T FEEL LIKE YOU NEED TO TALK ABOUT EVERYTHING TODAY, OKAY?
...
...
...
...
...
...

M-MAA-CHAN... YOU'RE THE ADULT HERE.
TAKE THE LEAD...
......
...DID YOU HEAR FROM THAT PERSON... KAWACHI-SAN...
...THAT *THE TRUTH IS THAT I WAS* YOUR MOTHER?
WELL...

HUH ...?
"I WAS" ...?
?
?
??

WELL... UM...
I...
DID WE MEET AFTER I WAS OLD ENOUGH TO UNDERSTAND WHAT WAS GOING ON?
I'M... SORRY...
I...
...I REMEMBER GRANDFATHER VAGUELY... AND I CAN REMEMBER SPECIFIC EVENTS, BUT...

...UM...
...IT'S LIKE, BEFORE I KNEW IT, I WAS LIVING WITH DAIKICHI...
HOW MUCH DO YOU REMEMBER ABOUT S-SOUICHI-SAN?
WELL, GRAND-PA...
...HE LOOKED A LOT LIKE DAIKICHI...
OH, WAIT. IT'S THAT DAIKICHI LOOKS LIKE HIM, RIGHT...?
...HE WAS A MAN OF FEW WORDS, I THINK.
WHEN I TOOK A NAP, HE'D PAT MY BACK...

BUT...
...MY MEMORIES OF THOSE TIMES...
...SOMETIMES I'M NOT EVEN SURE WHICH ONES WERE WITH GRANDPA...
...AND WHICH WERE WITH DAIKICHI.
GRANDPA LOVED THE RINDOU FLOWERS.
THERE WERE SO MANY GROWING IN THE GARDEN...
AND AT THE SAME TIME EVERY DAY, HE'D OPEN UP THE WALL CLOCK...
...AND WIND IT...

GRANDPA SAID, "INSTEAD OF DOING THAT..."
I WANTED TO DO IT TOO, BUT...
...I COULDN'T REACH IT, SO...
......
AH...
...WHAT WAS IT HE SAID TO DO INSTEAD ...?

A DAILY CALENDAR.
OH...
THAT'S RIGHT...
...HE PUT ME IN CHARGE OF THE DAILY CALENDAR...
HUH ...?
BUT WHY DO YOU —?

'COS I...
...WAS *THERE* TOO.
I WAS THERE WITH YOU UNTIL YOU WERE ABOUT FIVE.
WE LIVED TOGETHER.
WHAT ...?
WASN'T I LIVING WITH GRANDPA...?
YOU WERE.
TECHNI-CALLY, THE THREE OF US WERE LIVING TOGETHER.

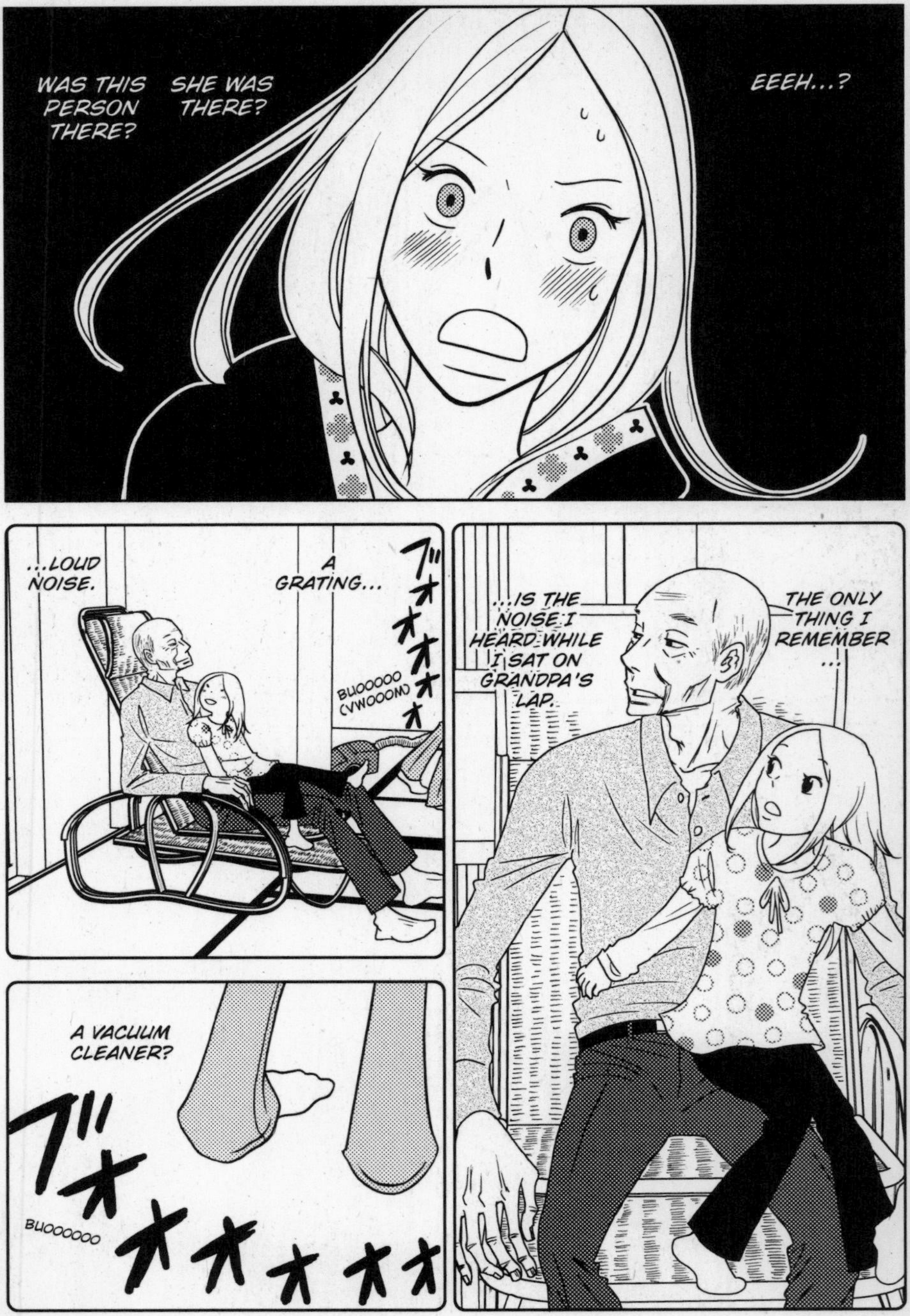
EEEH...?
SHE WAS THERE?
WAS THIS PERSON THERE?
THE ONLY THING I REMEMBER ...
...IS THE NOISE I HEARD WHILE I SAT ON GRANDPA'S LAP.
A GRATING...
...LOUD NOISE.
ブォオオオオオ
BUOOOOO (VWOOOM)
A VACUUM CLEANER?
ブォオオオオオオ
BUOOOOOO

I...
...I'M SORRY.
WELL, THAT'S ABOUT THE EXTENT OF A CHILD'S MEMORY, I GUESS.
MY MEMORY ISN'T ALL THAT CLEAR...
THAT...
...WAS MY "MOTHER"?
......
THIS GIRL ...
HER MEMORY JUST HAS GAPS WHERE MAA-CHAN'S CONCERNED ...?
WELL ...
SO...

I'M SORRY...
I JUST HAD... WORK THAT I REALLY NEEDED TO DO.
YOU MIGHT NOT UNDERSTAND MY REASONS NOW, BUT...
...AT THE TIME...
...I BE-LIEVED...
...THAT THERE WERE PLENTY OF PEOPLE WHO COULD BE "MOTHERS," BUT...
...THAT I WAS THE ONLY PERSON WHO COULD DO "MY WORK."

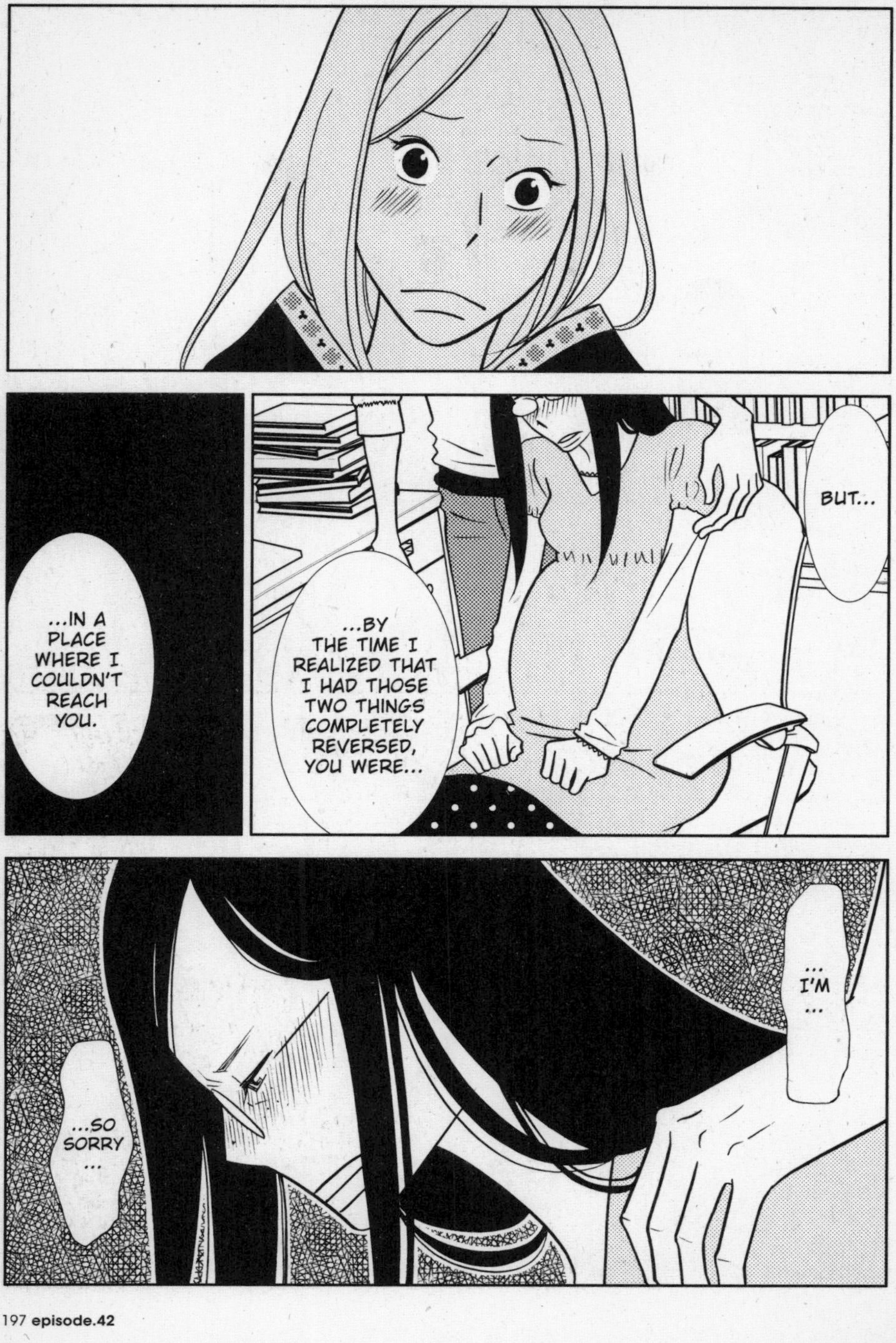
BUT...
...BY THE TIME I REALIZED THAT I HAD THOSE TWO THINGS COMPLETELY REVERSED, YOU WERE...
...IN A PLACE WHERE I COULDN'T REACH YOU.
...I'M...
...SO SORRY...

......
ギュ
GYU (SQUEEZE)
WHAT SHOULD I SAY...?
"DAIKICHI WAS LIKE A REAL FATHER TO ME.
"AND HE RAISED ME WELL."
IF I SAID THAT...
...WOULD SHE FEEL REASSURED...?
SAD...?
......
I DON'T KNOW...
I'LL JUST KEEP QUIET...

SIGN: RESTAURANT CHOMP
レストラン
RESTAURANT
ガブット
OPEN

HEY, NOW! YOU TWO MUST BE GETTING TIRED DOING ALL THIS TALKING AT ONCE...
...SO LET'S REST UP FOR ONE ROUND AND HAVE SOME TEA.
THANK YOU...
I'LL GLADLY HAVE SOME.
HAVE SOME SNACKS TOO.
WHAT!? WASN'T THERE ANYTHING ELSE? SHE'S IN HIGH SCHOOL...
OH, RIGHT...
AH!
IT'S OKAY. I LOVE TAIYAKI.

REALLY? I'M GLAD!
THESE ARE ONES THAT WERE BAKED ONE AT A TIME ON METAL MOLDS.
OH? THAT'S RARE THESE DAYS.
MAA-CHAN LOVES THESE TOO, SO I GET THEM A LOT.
LIKE MOTHER, LIKE DAUGHTER!
THERE ARE PLENTY OF PEOPLE WHO LIKE TAIYAKI.
OOH... MAA-CHAN, THERE YOU GO SAYING STUFF LIKE THAT AGAIN...
RUINING THE MOOD...
UM...
...IS THIS A STUDIO OR SOMETHING?
FOR A DESIGNER, MAYBE...?
NOPE, A MANGA ARTIST.

WHAT ...!?
R-R-REALLY?
MAA-CHAN IS.
MUGU (CHEW) むぐ MUGU むぐ
OH ...
?
I'VE NEVER SEEN A MANGA ARTIST IN PERSON BEFORE...

IT'S A GIRL ... ... PROB-ABLY ...
I'M DUE...
...NEXT MONTH.
......
SORRY ...
UM...

...THEN WOULD IT BE OKAY...
...TO THINK OF MYSELF AS A "BIG SISTER"?
!!
HUH ...?
......
UH...
I...
...GUESS YOU WOULD BE THAT...
DIFFER-ENT FATHER, THOUGH.
AGH... UNNECES-SARY COMMENT!

OH, THEN DOES THAT MEAN I CAN BE RIN-CHAN'S DAD?
UMM ...
I'M SORRY... THAT'S A LITTLE TOO MUCH... RIGHT NOW...
ID-IOT ...
THANK YOU FOR LETTING ME COME OVER.
I'M GLAD I GOT TO MEET YOU.
AH, I'LL WALK YOU OUT.

CAN I...
...GIVE YOU A HUG?

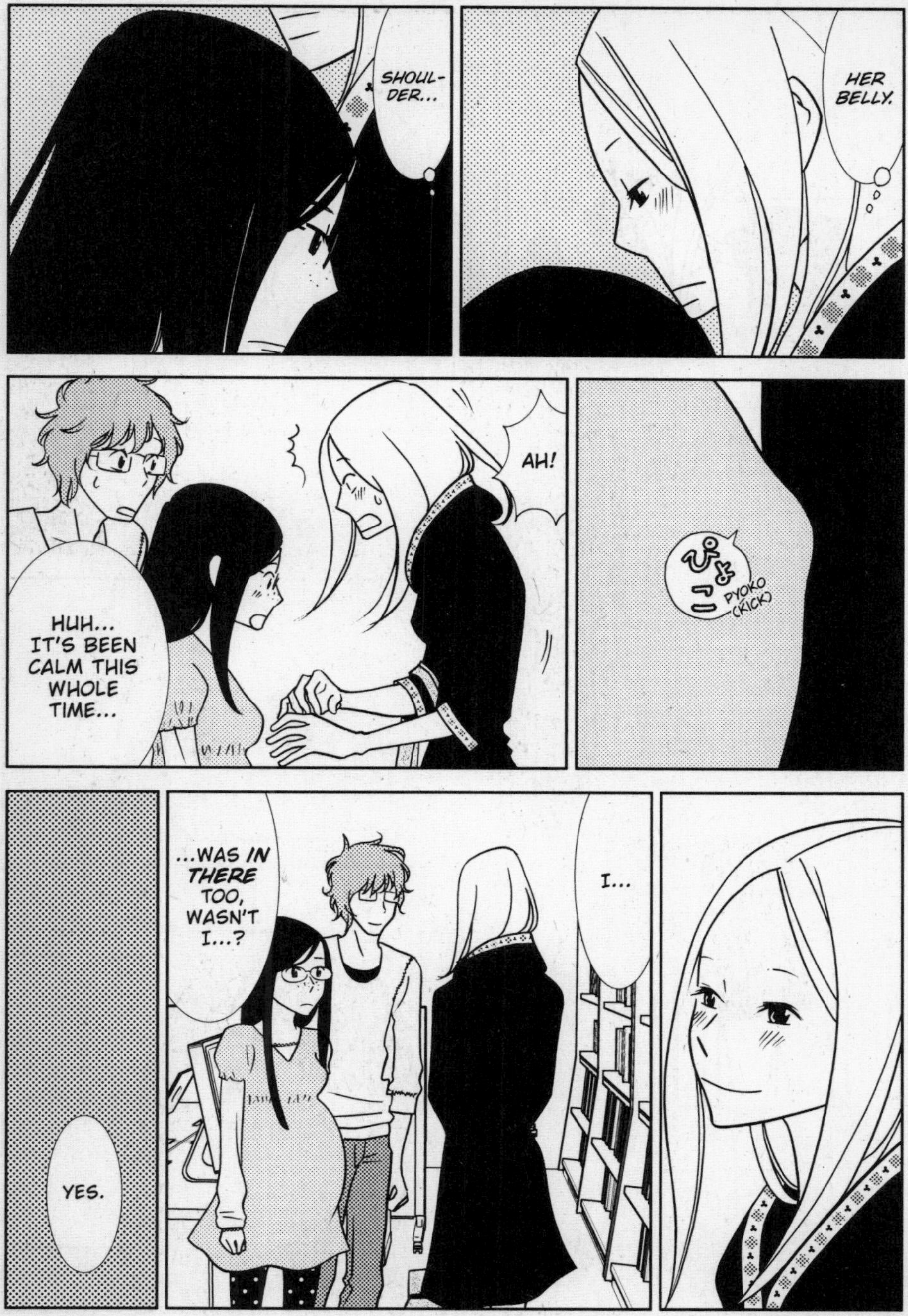
HER BELLY.
SHOUL-DER...
AH!
HUH... IT'S BEEN CALM THIS WHOLE TIME...
ぴょこ
PYOKO (KICK)
I...
...WAS *IN THERE* TOO, WASN'T I...?
YES.

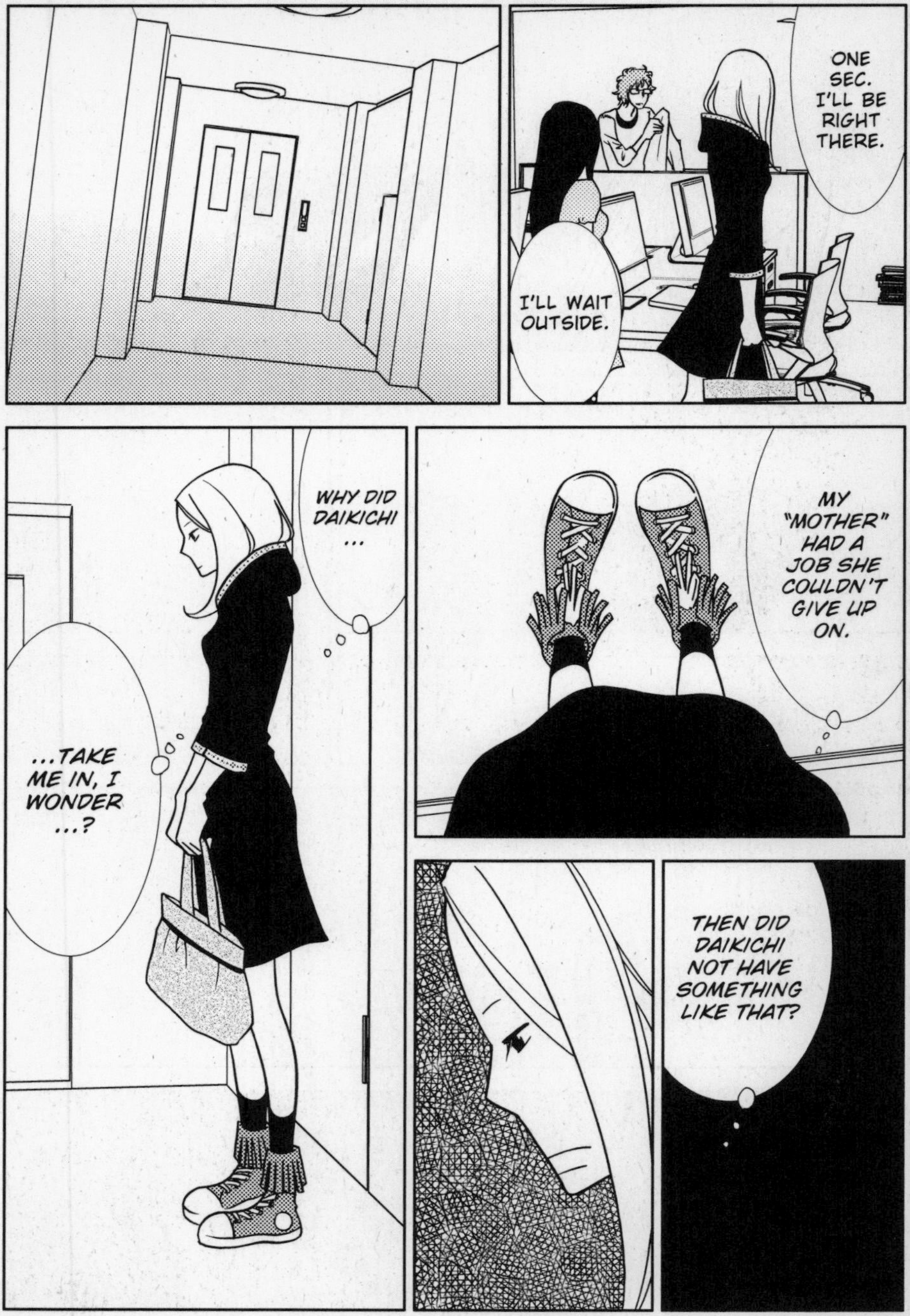
ONE SEC. I'LL BE RIGHT THERE.
I'LL WAIT OUTSIDE.
WHY DID DAIKICHI ...
...TAKE ME IN, I WONDER ...?
MY "MOTHER" HAD A JOB SHE COULDN'T GIVE UP ON.
THEN DID DAIKICHI NOT HAVE SOMETHING LIKE THAT?

WHY WAS IT DAIKICHI ...?
BUT IF SHE'D BEEN A GOOD PARENT AND HAD RAISED YOU WELL...
...THEN WE'D PROBABLY NEVER HAVE MET...
SO THAT POSSIBILITY DID EXIST.

BUT I DON'T LIKE THAT...
...EITHER.
BEING WITH DAI-KICHI...
...IS THE BEST...

to be continued...

TRANSLATION NOTES

COMMON HONORIFICS

No honorific: Indicates familiarity or closeness; if used without permission or reason, addressing someone in this manner would constitute an insult.

-san: The Japanese equivalent of Mr./Mrs./Miss. If a situation calls for politeness, this is the fail-safe honorific.

-kun: Used most often when referring to boys (though it can be applied to girls as well), this indicates affection or familiarity. Occasionally used by older men among their peers, but it may also be used by anyone referring to a person of lower standing.

-chan: An affectionate honorific indicating familiarity used mostly in reference to girls; also used in reference to cute persons or animals of either gender.

Page 9
Modanyaki: A variant of the savory Japanese *okonomiyaki* pancake (*okonomi*, which means "as you like it," and *yaki*, "grilled"). The ingredients, toppings, and method of cooking *okonomiyaki* vary by region, but the main version is the Kansai (Osaka) style with the ingredients mixed into the batter. In the southern (Hiroshima) style, the ingredients are layered and also include things like noodles and egg layers. The *modanyaki* pancake has a layer of fried noodles.

Page 11
Curryshtew: Here, Reina mispronounces the word *kareishuu*, a distinct body odor in older people caused by the increasing presence of the chemical nonenal on the skin's surface with age. The pronunciation of this word sounds similar to the pronunciation of "curry stew" in Japanese.

Page 31
"You can't pay out what you don't have, right?": In the original, this is *nai sode wa furenu*, a Japanese saying that states that one cannot swing sleeves one does not have, meaning that a person cannot give help to another when they themselves have nothing. This phrase originated in the Edo period when the poor, after selling everything else, would finally be forced to sell the sleeves from their kimono, meaning that they no longer had a place (like a pocket) to stash anything of value.

Page 57
Famicom: In Japan, the Nintendo Entertainment System was released in 1983 under the name "Family Computer" or "Famicom."

Page 58
Unagi Drop: A pun on the original title of *Bunny Drop* (*Usagi Drop*). *Unagi* is "sea urchin" in Japanese.

Page 79
Karaage: A Japanese cooking technique where food (generally meat) is marinated and fried. A popular *karaage* dish is chicken *karaage*, where the meat is marinated in a mix of soy sauce, garlic, ginger, and flour, then fried.

Page 96
Koseki: An official document under the Law of the Family Register that records names, dates of records (birth, marriage, death, adoption, etc.), and places. Typically each household has a koseki.

Page 101
Registered residence or address: On the *koseki*, this refers to the *honseki*, the place where one is registered and can be considered one's symbolic home. Individuals can still live in one town and retain their *koseki* in a different location, just as one can have a place they consider their true home, birthplace, current home, etc. The specific government office controlling the *koseki* is determined by the *honseki*.

Page 111

Resident registry: The *juuminhyou* is the document issued by the local government office indicating the address of an individual and can be requested to give evidence of one's *honseki-chi*, or permanent address. This document is generally only requested by the individual specified on the form and can be used for a variety of purposes (renewing visas, passports, etc).

Page 117

Postal money order: These are known as *teigakukogawase,* postal money orders that come in fixed amounts and can be purchased at any post office in Japan. This is typically the best way of sending money to pay for a document fee.

Page 200

Taiyaki: Fish-shaped pastry filled with sweet bean paste or other fillings.

Hello! This is YOTSUBA!

Guess what? Guess what?
Yotsuba and Daddy just moved here
from waaaay over there!

And Yotsuba met these
nice people next door and made
new friends to play with!

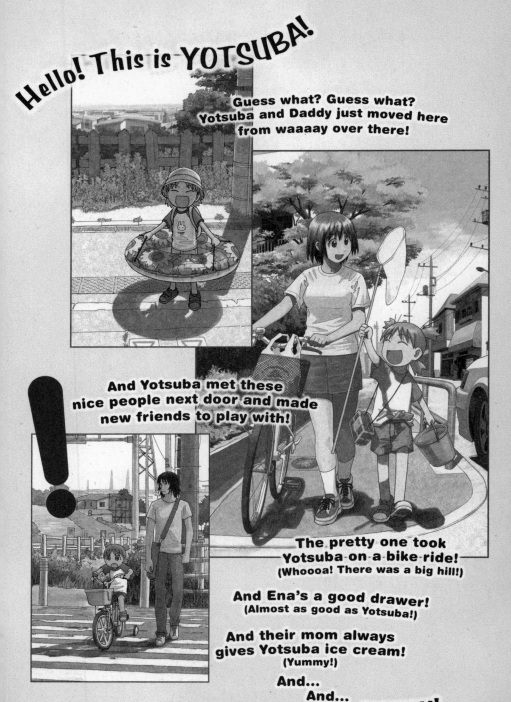

The pretty one took
Yotsuba on a bike ride!
(Whoooa! There was a big hill!)

And Ena's a good drawer!
(Almost as good as Yotsuba!)

And their mom always
gives Yotsuba ice cream!
(Yummy!)

And...
And...
OHHHH!

THE JOURNEY CONTINUES IN THE MANGA ADAPTATION OF THE HIT NOVEL SERIES
IN STORES NOW
SPICE & WOLF
MATURE
M
Spice and Wolf © Isuna Hasekura/Keito Koume/ASCII MEDIA WORKS

Yen Press
www.yenpress.com
Available at bookstores near you!
CHOCOLAT
1~7
Shin JiSang · Geo
Kum-ji was a little late getting under the spell of the chart-topping band, DDL. Unable to join the DDL fan club, she almost gives up on meeting her idols, until she develops a cunning plan–to become a member of a rival fan club for the brand-new boy band Yo-I. This way she can act as Yo-I's fan club member and also be near Yo-I,
How far would you go to meet your favorite boy band?
who always seem to be in the same shows as DDL. Perfect plan...except being a fanatic is a lot more complicated than she expects. Especially when you're actually a fan of someone else. This full-blown love comedy about a fan club will make you laugh, cry, and laugh some more.

BUNNY DROP 7

YUMI UNITA

Translation: Kaori Inoue • Lettering: Alexis Eckerman

Yen Press
Hachette Book Group
237 Park Avenue, New York, NY 10017

www.HachetteBookGroup.com
www.YenPress.com

Yen Press is an imprint of Hachette Book Group, Inc. The Yen Press name and logo are trademarks of Hachette Book Group, Inc.

First Yen Press Edition: November 2012

ISBN: 978-0-316-21720-0

10 9 8 7 6 5 4 3 2 1

BVG

Printed in the United States of America

BUNNYDROP
yumi unita